# FROM LAWYER

## *The Journe...*

MW01235123

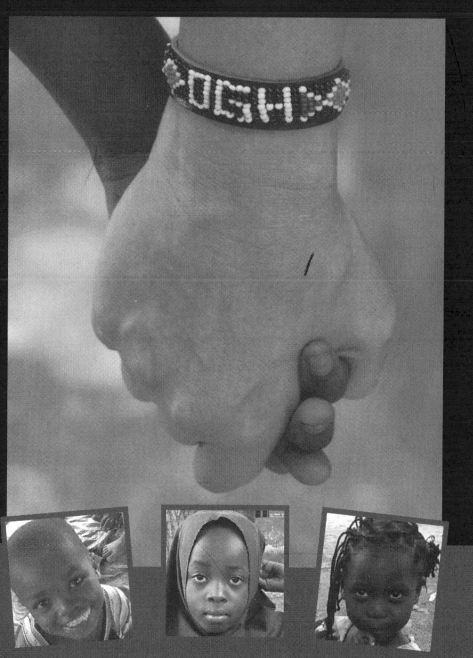

*By Carrie Reichartz*

## *This book is dedicated to...*

My husband Chris, my mom, my dad, and my kids, Colton
and Brooklyn. Without their help, I could never do what I do,
including raising money, helping at rummage sales, with the kids,
and just being supportive financially and physically.

*Thanks for all you do to make this possible.*

On the Kenyan side, I dedicate this book to Jim and Susie Horne–
without their dedication to the children and people of Kenya and their
constant presence in that country, none of this work would be as strong
as it is. They are there, right next to the locations in which we serve,
not some other part of the country. They visit the schools weekly,
encouraging our staff, and the churches they are involved with,
to strive to be more for God everyday.

*Thank you for your tremendous examples.*

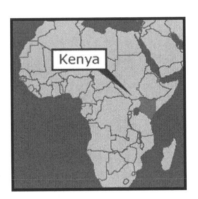

*Special prayers to Robert and Iman Lundi and O'neal.*
*God is with you on this journey.*

Published in 2016

www.fromlawyertomissionary.com
www.kenyagivehope.com

ISBN 10 1542486904
ISBN 13 9781542486903

**About the cover:**
*Photo by Jesi Epsie. Carrie holding hands with Mwanarusi Rashid, the girl
who stole her heart and brought Carrie back to Kenya again and again in
Tiwi, Kenya.*

# CONTENTS

## Chapter 4

## Chapter 5

## Chapter 6

## *Chapter 10*

# ACKNOWLEDGEMENTS

I don't even know where to begin. This project has taken several years of edits, revisions, writing, re-writing, graphics, with trips to Kenya and life in between.

I am very afraid of leaving someone out. So first – anyone and everyone that had anything to do with this project I thank you so much.

*Maddy Lamers* for her initial edit of the book

*Becky Melby and Jen Miller* for a middle edit of the book

*Andrew Maul* all the way from half-way around the world for the final edit prior to production of the book

*Friends, family, Beth and Diana* for the proofing of the book before it went to print

*Mary Lange* for her tireless help in the graphic layout of this book inside and out

*Ashley Lamba* for reformatting our Kenyan stories for that chapter of the book

*Charlie Evans* for his encouragement, financial support, edits, hints and dedication to writing

*My family – husband Chris* for his patience when I spend a full week writing and all his help and support

*My mom – Connie Randlett* for all her support in so many ways

*All of the amazing Kenyan friends* that have helped make trips possible and keep the work going

*All the tireless volunteers* that have come on trips with us, that have helped at events, that have helped with other tasks behind the scene.

Thank you all. Without your help, none of what is taking place would be possible!

*Thank you, thank you, thank you!*

# INTRODUCTION

Thank you for coming along on part two of this journey From Lawyer to Missionary. First I want to thank you. Just by purchasing this book, you have made a difference in the lives of people in Kenya. By sharing the book, and the experiences within it, you can take the work even further! Thank you for all the support, in every way you give it!

Since the last book, I hope you have taken some time to figure out where you are making a difference in the world. I want these books to be about us making a difference together. I would love to hear stories of the differences being made in your lives. Visit me by going on the websites listed in the back of this book and share your stories. Those stories help me keep moving forward with God, just as I hope this story will help you.

I can hardly remember where we left off, as so much has happened in Kenya, and in me, since we last came together.

*Come along on the next steps in this amazing journey!*

*Chapter 1*

# Financial Worries – They Are Never What They Seem

## NOW WHERE WERE WE?

In our last travels we talked about all the work we were doing with the children of Kenya:

- Visiting and helping with various projects at government schools, organizing a library, donating pencils, pens, paper, and desks;
- Speaking at various girls' high schools in Kenya—especially focusing on their dreams and on school, instead of on boys -- and how getting pregnant would affect their dreams;
- Spending time at orphanages and children's homes in Mombasa, Kenya with Sue Huerta specifically at Peter and Selpher Mutua's Baby Life Rescue Center.
- Encouraging various women's groups in Vipingo and Bomani, both spiritually and financially, by providing seed money for them to start opportunities to make money;

We also spoke of the work in developing a sponsorship program for our Operation Give Hope schools in Kenya, which provides high quality education, two meals daily, water, and more, for only $25 per month. This is much more than other sponsorship programs are able to provide, at almost half the cost.

We are able to do so much for such a low dollar amount for two reasons:

First, we are focusing in one geographical area, and have been there long-term, so we can use our knowledge and leverage. Second, we have close to zero dollars being spent in overhead expenses. Our board, and friends of our board, are extremely generous in all the donations they make with in-kind donations of postage and stamps, and other donated expenses. We try to pay our accountants, but a lot of them put their funds right back into the account to be used for the kids. I am so glad to be working with people that are doing this for God, not for recognition or money.

We left off our last journey working with a Kenyan lawyer, Vicky, and Helen, Kenyan psychologist, in April, 2012, with the kickoff of our adoption work in Kenya through Pilgrim's Adoption Resource Center.

*Now, let's see where God takes us next!*

## RETURNING HOME, APRIL 2012

Upon arriving home, Sue Huerta (a frequent co-traveler) and I had committed to meeting weekly to pray for and discuss Kenya, what more we could do for Kenya, and possible future trips. Sue and I developed quite a list of things to do, and a list of items that were needed for the orphanages and the other places we had visited. We had long lists, but most were quite simple and doable. The challenge would be shipping everything over to Kenya once collected. We looked into the cost of shipping and the smallest container available was going to run $5,500. That left us discouraged, but we kept believing that God would provide the answer.

After sharing our shipping struggles, Fox River Christian Church in Waukesha generously asked if we would like to have some space in a container they were shipping over to Kenya in late 2012 or early 2013. We jumped at the chance. God is good. Keep moving forward and He provides a way!

So we started our quest for baby items for the orphanages in Mombasa. We were able to get a specific wish list from the people that run Baby Life Rescue, the orphanage we visit every time we are in Kenya. They label it their "faith list". Peter and Selpher Mutua run the center where they do a lot of domestic adoptions. They gave us a list to work on, and Sue and I added in baby items such as Exersaucers and Bumbo™ chairs that people living in Kenya wouldn't even know about.

Given that Sue and I both run day cares and frequent rummage sale and resale shops, it couldn't be too hard to do, but wait to see what God had planned!

## LIFE IS ABOUT RELATIONSHIPS

Sue and I enjoyed our get-togethers. It was a perfect example of life being about relationship. Though we would talk about and pray for Kenya, we would talk more about our lives and encourage each other.

A lot of changes were going on in Sue's life with her business. She was stepping back a little bit from some of the daily work. With her relationship with God, she was trying to figure out where He was leading her. I had various struggles with parenting and life in general, but we were able to keep moving forward together, even through some struggles. We would just share our lives with each other which helped each of us see things in a clearer perspective.

Kenya has taught me so much about what is really important in life. I tend to be more task oriented. Making enough money is important. Having a working car is important. Getting a new outfit is important sometimes... the list could go on and on.

## NEW RELATIONSHIPS FILLING CURRENT NEEDS?

During this time, I read in the Hales Corners Lutheran Church bulletin that the Lutheran Women's Missionary League would be holding their project planning meeting for the following year.

As a missionary myself, I was very excited to see what this group was doing. So I decided to go to the meeting and was fortunate enough to share with them some of the things I had been doing in Kenya.

Together we planned what projects would be done for each month of the following year. For instance, one month we would pack and ship boxes of little stuff to military stationed overseas. Another month we would host donation boxes to take to various women's shelters. We assigned a project to every month except for two.

By this time, I had long stopped focusing just on Kenya. As Divine intervention would have it, while brainstorming ideas for these last two months, another group member suggested having a presentation about Kenya. The group was excited, and I was thrilled to have the opportunity to get the Operation Give Hope name out to even more people. It's funny how sometimes answers come to you when you stop looking for them.

My focus of previous presentations had been on raising money to build an adoption center in Kenya, and to support kids at the school. So I didn't feel that it was the right fit for this time to pray about what type of presentation to give. I needed to come at the event with a new approach, but didn't quite know how to do that.

After a few weeks of prayer, an idea came into my mind to host a "Kenyan Baby Shower Event". Ladies could come with financial donations, or items off our list of needs for the orphanages, and also raise awareness of all what Operation Give Hope is doing in Kenya. At the same time, we could share a few travel stories of the trips over the last few years and play a few "shower" games as ice breakers.

It was a whole new approach, and I was excited to pull it all together. I always love a baby shower! This event was the motivating factor to get me going on the first book. A very small outline of the book was what I ended up using as the presentation for the event.

It is so fun to look back at all the needs God covers through unique and new ways every time!

## ORGANIZING FOR NEXT TRIP

During this time, we were also finalizing our plans for the next trip to Kenya scheduled for June, 2012. I was going with Ken Kernen who attends Risen Savior Lutheran Church in Franklin, Wisconsin. A friend of mine, Kristen, who has done extensive work in Kenya, had another friend that helped fundraise for some mosquito netting a few years back, when she was living in Kenya for three months. Ken has had a deep passion for Kenya ever since hearing about Kristen's work there.

Ken and I had been meeting for several years to determine the best plan and timing for a trip. He had a few things get in the way of other trips—loss of a job and other things—but here it was, his first trip.

Ken's dream is for his church to sponsor a school in Kenya, similar to how Fox River is sponsoring schools. He has a very, very small church, but they seemed like they might be ready to jump on board and help the people of Kenya.

Ken and I were planning to go to Kenya almost a week earlier than the rest of the group so we could check out some places he and his church might be able to support, similar to our school.

## SHOW ME THE MONEY!

I am learning there is always a trip before the trip. In March 2012, I was physically struggling, having a 103 degree fever only two hours before leaving. This time it was financial worry, though I am learning more and more that financial struggles are not really about money -- they are more about the emotional and mental energy focused on the financial struggle. Read on for an example of what I mean!

First, the problem. Or should I say, *problems!* It was Monday, the 4th of June. We were scheduled to leave in a little over a week. We had just had our last fund raiser and had raised about $500. After expenses, that still left me with a $1,200 shortfall. Strike one.

Oh,wait, did I forget to mention that my 16-year-old had an "incident" with my car that weekend that left the side impact airbags deployed? Oh, yes, that and some other damage, though no other cars or property were involved, thankfully. That was at least a $1,000 deductible, as well as future increases in car insurance, which had already increased with him being put on the policy. Strike two and maybe three.

Then I got final grades for my son's report card. He had been attending Milwaukee Lutheran, a private school, that year. The school is great, but he was not enjoying it. The deal was if he got good grades – C's or better in every class - he could return to New Berlin public schools the next year.

Well, I knew he got a D in religion and after some discussions with some friends I was willing to overlook that grade in our deal. As life is not about religion *for* God, it's about a relationship *with* God, I was set to go home to tell him he could return to the public school next year which is free for me. Then I read my emails. He got a D in English too. Is God saying he belongs at Milwaukee Lutheran again? That will be $9,000 please! Strike three.

Then as we approached 4:00 p.m. on that beautiful Monday, the day care parents are coming to pick up their children, which is always a very busy time. Well, this particular day it was exceptionally "exciting" for me, as two parents, one with two kids, and another with one, came in to inform me that they were moving or that their job had changed. My day care services would no longer be needed as it was too far out of the way for their new ventures. They loved the service they were getting, but location was not working. Strike four. I am more than out.

Okay, let's get this straight. We've got over $11,000 in expenses and now my income is being cut by almost $1,600 per month, all in one day? And some of that is needed next week to leave on a trip that has been planned for over a year. Can you say financial worry?

I've been through financial struggles before and I know God has pulled me out of them by His grace, but this was too much for me. It felt like this was too much for God too.

Negative thoughts were spiraling all around my head. How am I going to do this? This is just too much and not enough time to do it in. After three days of constant stress and complaining to anyone that would listen, I woke up at midnight and felt the stress immediately. Then, in that moment, the thought came to my mind -- I am focusing way too much on *me* and not enough on *God*. If I stepped down from the middle of my life for a minute and let God take over and put those things into perspective, my life would go back to being peaceful. In that moment, that was exactly what I did. I gave it over to God to handle while I fell right back to sleep.

I woke up the next morning as a whole new me. I was not stressed. I was not worried. I knew it was God's problem to figure out and I could just sit back and do what He told me to do. So, that's what I did. I got up and ran my three-mile morning run. Then, I came home, showered, and did my 30 minutes of time with God in the morning. Once I was done with that, God showed me exactly where to find the money for the rest of the trip to Kenya. It was sitting right there in my kitchen in some envelopes, but I was so stressed I couldn't even see that.

Dave Ramsey has a budget idea of putting money into envelopes to spend on certain things, and when the money is gone it is gone. You cannot spend anymore in that area. As I would be out of the country for two weeks,

I wouldn't be spending any money on my usual expenses here at home. Therefore, that money would be available to take with me to Kenya, and it just happened to be the $1,200 I needed. Okay – strike one was gone and God had it covered within hours.

Then, later that day, I was reading, preparing my heart for Kenya, and God reminded me that my son had some money coming in the middle of the month. That would be more than enough to cover the deductible for the car damage.

All I had to do was step back and let go of the negative mental and emotional energy I was expending and God could put thoughts in my mind to solve the problem. Strike two gone — God had it covered.

The other two took a few more weeks to resolve, but nonetheless, God took care of them, one-by-one. I was open to seeing God working, and open to where God was showing me to get the money. Sure enough, everything fell right into place, and there was no extra work involved. All the funds were right there in front of me, but my mental and emotional strain over the situation had blinded me. When I let go and let God lead me, the funds showed up— "oh ye of little faith". It's unbelievable when I think about it, but it is true.

If this is what God is showing me while still at home, what has He planned for the trip? Let's find out.

*Chapter 2*

# Things Don't Always Go Smoothly
## June 2012: Ken and Carrie

I got up, ran two miles, and did my morning readings. It was a day like any other. I worked a full day and said some hard, long-term goodbyes to a few day care kids that would be leaving while we were away on the trip. I enjoyed checking Facebook for farewell wishes, and spent some time with my daughter. I was very ready to go and felt fully prepared after the extra time spent with God in the last week over the financial issues. I was ready to get away and get perspective, and see what God had in store for us next. I will miss my family during this trip. My husband and son have been gone since Sunday on their summer vacations. This is an extra long trip for me, two and a half weeks, rather than two.

Ken Kernen arrived at 5:00 pm to load the truck and head out. The trip to the airport was uneventful. We stopped at Panda Express, my favorite, for dinner. Somehow, we managed not to hit any traffic heading down through Chicago. We got the luggage together and paid another $220 for extra baggage fees, but we were ready for that this time. The plane took off at 10:20pm, and landed on time. We were off to a great start!

On the first flight, I could not even keep my eyes open through the safety presentation. I was asleep before we left the gate. We arrived at the Istanbul airport in Turkey for a 2 hour and 45 minute layover, but we were at the way back of the plane, second to last seats, so were out in perfect time to just about walk directly onto the next flight. I have to say I love Turkish Airlines.

## SMOOTHLY? NOT SO MUCH

On the second flight, our plane had three seats across on the sides and four seats across in the middle, so it was not easy to get up and access the aisle. I could not get back to sleep at all after the person in the middle seat needed to get up 10 minutes into my nap. Therefore, I decided to work on my writing—this is when I started the first book—*From Lawyer to Missionary: A Journey to Kenya and Back Again.*

We arrived in Nairobi on June 14, 2012 at 2:45 am. We found our most important bags for the beginning of the trip, but one was missing. Trying to report lost luggage along with 50 other people at 2:45 am was not a fun task. I had a meeting with a children's law and constitutional law lawyer at 11:00 am, so every minute at the airport meant less sleep, which meant money wasted on the hotel.

Once the luggage issue was dealt with, a bigger problem emerged. We couldn't find the person who was supposed to be picking us up from the airport. So there we were, stranded at the airport, at 4:00 am. Yikes! I was glad I had a man with me on this trip.

After asking around and wandering for awhile, we got a ride from another taxi driver. Once at the hotel, I tried to figure out how to get in contact with our driver as he was also supposed to be our driver that weekend while we were in Nairobi. Needless to say, we never did find him.

By the time we got in and somewhat organized for the next day, it was very close to 6:00 am. It would be getting light within 30 minutes. We had to eat breakfast by 9:00 am. There were other mission groups near us that were up early doing their daily meeting. These took place right outside my door, so it was quite a morning. So, no driver and not a lot of sleep.

I was finally able to figure out a taxi for the day, and we were off to meet Bobby, the children's law lawyer, but not before our taxi ran out of gas. The driver pulled up onto the curb for a few blocks to try to tilt the gas to the best part of the car to keep moving -- apparently he had been in this position before! A block before the final destination he asked if we could walk the rest of the way, and pointed out the spot while he took care of the gas problem.

## CHILDREN'S LAW LAWYER IN NAIROBI

Bobby is actually a cousin to two people I introduced you to in the last book: Allan, a Kenyan who lives in South Milwaukee, and Tito, the Kenyan who runs a school in Ribe who we helped organize a library for at Carroll University in Waukesha, Wisconsin. I had been wanting to meet with him for several years and was so grateful that we were finally able to set it up.

Bobby was great. He was able to tell us about various ongoing adoptions, and kids that were sponsored by UNICEF and the Kenyan government. The adoption laws in Kenya are only ten years old. This is hard to imagine - only ten years old! But now that they have a ten-year track record, they want to review their placements and laws to see what kind of changes they might be able to implement to make the process easier, and better, for parents and kids.

Bobby felt that after this study was complete, the time would be perfect for looking into changing the existing three month waiting period for adoption cases (which can easily turn into two years). The way it works, the parents come and bond with the child for three months. After that period the parents are free to leave, but without the child. They must stay in Kenya if they want to be with the child, pending the full adoption hearing.

We talked about the reasoning behind the waiting period for international adoption. The waiting period exists to assess the bonding of parents to children and to give the social workers time to do their work. He indicated that the government would probably be willing to address the issue again and look at other options. He felt the biggest stumbling block would be the cost of returning a child if the adoption is not finalized. That was very encouraging, as I would like to see international adoption expanded in Kenya, to the United States, and around the world.

Bobby is at this moment writing and speaking about children's rights under the new Kenyan constitution and looking for test cases to set base lines. He feels, and I agree, that education, water, and food rights for kids are imperative to getting a step ahead for the children of Kenya. He is studying South Africa as a role model.

## LUTHERAN MISSIONARIES IN NAIROBI

In order to not be two hours late (like the last visit), we headed right to the Lutheran missionary's house of Shauen and Krista Trump. We arrived one hour early, so we just walked around their compound and enjoyed nature and the beautiful gardens. It is a quiet, peaceful area a little outside of Nairobi, in a city called Karen.

First, we got a chance to see Shauen's office and how he kept track of all his Lutheran mission groups that come for various trips to various areas. Then, we headed back to the house for dessert and tea with his wife Krista.

Shauen educated us on Kenyan culture and schooling. Some of which I already knew, but it's always good to hear it again and gain further understanding. Their school system runs more like a British system than American, though there are probably lots of differences to the British system as well.

They have KG-1, KG-2, KG-3. These are the kindergarten classes, similar to our preschool through kindergarten. They have classes for Standard 1, 2, 3, 4, 5, 6, 7, 8. This is like our grades, though the kids don't understand when we ask what grade are you in —they assume we are asking them about their marks (grades) like on report cards. They only understand if you ask them what class they are in, and then they will tell you.

When they reach Standard 8, students take a standardized test (like our ACT or SAT). If they don't pass the standardized test they cannot move on to any further schooling. They do have the chance to take it again, but it is very difficult.

If you pass your Standard 8 exam at a really low level, you can only go on to a local school. They are not great schools, but at least it is some education. Hopefully, they can improve and get better at testing once they complete their four years of what we would call high school. They call it Form 1, 2, 3, 4. If they do pretty well on their class eight exam, they can test into district level schools. They are the second best schools in the country. The students with the highest test scores go to National Schools which are the best in the country.

Almost all of our Operation Give Hope school kids test into the top two level schools. Only the top few students of every district are able to test into a national school.

At Tiwi (one of our Operation Give Hope schools), we had one child that was the highest score in the entire district. At this point, I believe the government pays for the fees of the child. That shows the high quality the teaching and education is at our schools. We have many of our students that test into the top 20 list of the district level testing.

The problem for many students is that, even if they are able to pass into high school, they are not able to afford school fees at high school level, and are therefore not able to move on unless they get financial assistance. Currently, at Operation Give Hope, we only focus up to Standard 8.

We are hoping, at some point, someone might set up a program for funding high school expenses for at least the highest performing kids in the schools. The fees can be as minimal as $300 per year for a boarding school, which almost all high schools are in Kenya. It could easily be added to our sponsorship program if someone was willing to do the fund raising part of it. However, we do not currently have this opportunity for our kids.

Originally, Ken Kernen and I came up with the idea that he would work with a Lutheran missionary to support an Operation Give Hope preschool called Tumaini (Swahili for hope). This is the place where we previously had the water issues with the pond and filthy water and were able to provide a well. Coming here, a preschool was the direction we were heading.

I had spent a lot of time praying that both Ken and I would keep an open mind on where God was leading Ken and his church. It was hard because I had put a lot of time and energy into the organization of this trip and I wanted it to "pay it off" by having another Operation Give Hope school fully funded.

But in my prayers prior to the trip, I realized that whether Ken did or did not work with an Operation Give Hope school didn't matter. All that mattered was that we followed where God wanted us to go. If we did end up partnering in funding an Operation Give Hope school and it wasn't God's plan, it would end up falling apart anyway. That was a heavy, self-imposed weight lifted before we left, and I was grateful for that because of what was soon to come.

We had hours of discussion with Shauen and his wife on so many topics: school information, their family, life in Kenya, and so much more. At one point in our discussions with Shauen, the thought came up that maybe a secondary school (high school) would be a better option than a primary school. It was just a passing thought, and we moved on to the next topic in our very long discussions.

Then, at about 4:30 pm, the Lutheran bishop of the area came to Shauen's place with his project manager. Shauen had set this up after my last meeting with him in Kenya. It was a miracle to get them there all together in one place at one time. We discussed some of the works that we had done, and what we were hoping to do. The bishop asked if we were open to looking into a secondary school on South Coast. We told him that we had actually come thinking a primary school on South Coast, and that the thought of a secondary school came up just an hour before in our discussion with Shauen. Thanks to previous prayers, we were open to seeing that as a sign of where God wanted Ken and his church to proceed.

From there, they got us in telephone contact with Elias, the main person running their South Coast work, and we set up a meeting for Sunday. We were going to view the Lutheran primary school and orphanage, Faraha Children's Home, which had 10 or more acres around it.

All of this came about in a 30-minute meeting. In Kenyan time, no meetings are ever 30 minutes long! In Kenya, the first 30 minutes are often spent catching up —getting to know about the kids and family and life in general. Then, after 30 minutes, you can start to talk about some business, but very slowly. Almost every meeting, even the shortest of meetings, are two hours long. We were able to get through all of this info in just 30 minutes, and then they left, very quickly.

## NAIROBI MINISTRIES - BENTA AND NEW LIFE RESCUE

The next day, we were meeting Benta. You may remember her from the end of the last book and our days in Nairobi. She runs the HIV clinic where she educates moms, especially pregnant moms, about antiviral medicines and other things that can help them and their babies. Babies born with HIV can be positive at birth and turn to HIV negative if they receive the antiviral medicine promptly.

She sells various items (necklaces, purses, bracelets, banana prints, etc.) that the women make to help support the work. I bring home a lot of her stuff and sell it to raise money for the adoption work we are doing. It supports two awesome causes, and supporters get amazing one-of-a-kind, African pictures and purses. After some time with Benta, we were off to an orphanage.

I was hoping to be able to visit two orphanages, but that would have made it far too rushed. We settled on one, which was very close to the hotel where we were staying. The name of the orphanage - New Life Home Trust - is one of the oldest and most well known orphanages in the area. It was great to see. They have an excellent system and work hard on getting the children adopted out. Children are assigned to different rooms based on age. Once the kids turn three, they are moved to another New Life Home in Nairobi.

The kids were amazing! We started in the one-year-old room where the kids were just learning to walk, talk, and crawl. They were literally climbing the walls! After that, we went outside with the two-year-olds who were running the show with a ton of toys, inside and out. Then we went in to help feed the four to nine month old babies, and the two year olds, who made a huge mess.

I enjoyed getting to know one-year-old Sean, who I could not believe had not been adopted yet. He was the cutest little boy. He had a little trouble-maker personality, but one that you couldn't help but love. And Anthony, another one-year-old, with the same cute face, who was very quiet and determined. Julia, who was two, and very little and cute, but probably very sick because of her size. My guess is she had HIV, but I don't know her story. She had a very hard time eating. And there was Jerob, who was also two, and adorable.

Our taxi driver also got involved, pushing the kids around outside and having a good time. I got to feed six-month-old Roy, who looked like he could not be a day over four months, as he was so little. But he did well in the Bumbo chair I put him in when we went to feed the two-year-olds.

As you can probably tell from the names, there are a lot more boys in the orphanages than girls, especially in Nairobi where the actual adoptions take place. The ratio in the rooms we visited was one girl to every twelve boys. Girls are usually the first to be adopted. There are various reasons for this according to the staff and local people I spoke with.

First of all, if a single woman wants to adopt, she would have to adopt a girl. They will not allow a single woman to adopt a boy, and a single man is not allowed to adopt at all. Second, a family is less likely to give up a baby girl for adoption as they know that, at some point, a dowry for marriage would need to be exchanged. This is hope for money to solve some of their poverty. Third, if a family wanted to adopt a boy, they have to be prepared to give a dowry and land for the new couple to live on. To avoid that trouble, people tended to chose girls. I'm sure there were other reasons as well, but it is truly sad to see so many boys living in orphanages.

23

Ken and I had a great time at the orphanage. Ken was surprised at how interactive he was with the little ones. He has three sons, all of which were in their 20's at that point, and he indicated that, in the states in a situation like this, he would not have interacted as much as he did here. It is funny how you jump outside of your comfort zone so quickly when you're on a mission from God.

If I were running an orphanage, I would run it more like a family setting—various kids, at various ages, living together, and not moving them to a different home. New Life Home is doing wonderful work, taking in babies that were left in pit latrines or on the side of the road, abandoned, and nursing them back to health, loving them lots in the process. There were a lot of volunteers there to help the staff with all the children, and a wonderful nurse in charge—Charlene.

Now we are back to our running car. We spent quite a few hours at the orphanage and most of that time our driver was in the car listening to the radio. When we got to the car to head off to the airport, the car wouldn't start—the battery was dead. The driver called his friend for a literal human jump start of the taxi's battery. The driver's friend held onto each battery part while standing on the bumpers of both cars to jump start our taxi!

Unfortunately, at this point we were still minus one bag, and ironically we ran into problems with Kenya Airways wanting to charge us for extra bags from Nairobi to Mombasa. Last trip I was ready for that, but didn't have to pay so I didn't budget for it this trip. They wanted over $100 which we were not expecting. Though I was frustrated, we did pay the reduced fee of $41 and were on our way and on time, which was awesome. It is only a 45-minute flight from Nairobi to Mombasa.

## ADOPTION?

Playing with Sean rekindled a deep desire in my heart to possibly adopt some day. Though that would not be my personal desire to start over with a little one, as our children were then 14, 14, and 16. We had three teenagers at home! We were almost "free". I fought and fought with God over this as He kept bringing people, situations, stories, and guidance leading me toward adoption.

I have had a few dreams since this visit of adopting twin boys from Kenya. The problem is that in international adoption, you cannot pre-select the child or children you want to adopt. You fill out all the US forms and all the foreign country forms and then they forward you a list of a few children, their pictures, and their information. Then you can decide which ones you would like to meet. You cannot go into an orphanage in a foreign country and "baby shop" and then go home and start filling out the paperwork for a specific child. There are various reasons for this, including child trafficking and other safety issues. That's a possible God directive I'm not really sure how to jump into without being fully sure of every step up front. I will be continuing to pray about this and see where God leads me.

This was one incident, of quite a few over the last few months, leading to a pull for adoption. After a long struggle with God over the issue, finally, in October 2012, I was able to say, "I would love to adopt". This was after a year-long battle with God where I refused to accept that He might be calling our family to consider international adoption. It all started in January 2012, when my husband and I were doing a Bible study called "Experiencing God" by Henry Blackby. It is an amazing study, and every time I do the study it feels like I'm taking it for the first time. I would highly recommend it for everyone! Every time international adoption came up in the study, I attributed it to the work going on in Kenya.

Finally, I had a "come to Jesus moment" in my own bathroom mirror back home in the US (a moment God usually reserves for the hotel bathrooms in Kenya) after finally having the guts to share with two close friends about the struggle. I finally let go enough to see that if God wanted our family to adopt, even if it was not what I would consider good timing or the right decision, if it was His plan, it would be the right one. It seems so simple, but man that was a hard one!

You would think that was the hardest part, but wait, there's more! Even though it was so difficult to come to the decision to follow through on what God was calling me to do, now I had a family to discuss it with. I was finally on board and willing to do whatever God calls. I brought it up with my husband, and he was not on board. He had the same thoughts that I had. We were almost "free". The teenagers were enough work and he didn't want to go through that work again.

I was finding that even harder. I knew what God was calling our family to do, but not being able to do it, because my husband was not on board. Chris and I did attend an adoption informational class, but it wasn't really going anywhere and it had been a year. I thoroughly researched areas in which to adopt. I prayed about it. I printed off paperwork and started collecting documents, hoping God would change Chris' heart quickly. Then we would be ready. I came to the point of "waiting" without doing anything. It is hard, once you are ready to move forward, to not be able to even though you know in your heart it is God's plan. I think the hardest part is thinking about the child that God has chosen for us sitting there waiting for us and we are not there. That being said, though Chris is not on board for now, God can and will move large mountains to make it happen if it is His plan. So for now, we will wait and see!

## MOMBASA

We were happy to see Rashid at the airport to pick us up. Finally a familiar face! Rashid has been my driver for every trip in Kenya since 2008. He picked us up, and then we headed over to the missionary home of Jim and Susie Horne to pick up bags I had left from the last trip for our activity in Tiwi in a few days.

Thank you, George! He is always so very helpful. George is a person who works for Jim and Susie in many ways. He does things for the house, things for the church, helps with cultural issues, etc. He was so helpful in getting all the stuff together so we were all ready to go. With all nine suitcases and some extra bags of stuff, we arrived at the hotel. I had to get all the bags organized with all the stuff we needed for the activity day at Tiwi.

I expected my Kenyan phone to be waiting for me at the hotel so I could call my friends to have dinner and help organize, but no phone. Just add that to the list of little mishaps so far on the trip —no driver at the airport and we were never able to track him down, running out of gas on the way to our first meeting, needing a human jump-start to get to the airport. Thank God for Liz!

Liz works for Operation Give Hope on the Kenyan side doing all the accounting, photo updates, website info, and so many other things. She works so hard and does such amazing work. God sent her to help me get everything at least somewhat organized, and we were able to have some girl talk for a little while. It was so great to see her! She just showed up, paid for a cab ride to get there, hoped that I would be there, and I was! I was so happy to see her smiling face, and get her help.

We had the bags organized pretty quickly. As we were only to be in this hotel room for one night we had to unpack everything, get it into the right bag, and then repack everything. There was a lot of stuff for the orphanages

—little toys, baby boy clothes, my clothes, Tiwi activity stuff, shoes, more clothes to give away at Tiwi, and so many other things. It would have been a mess without Liz to help. She had been in Italy for almost a month and had just gotten back a week or so ago, so she was really busy trying to catch up on her work and get things back in order after being gone so long. She stayed for a while and then was on her way to get ready to go the next day to South Coast with us for the events we had planned there.

We decided to hit Ingili; Swahili for "Good News", a small village church, before church service so we could say hello to Pastor Allan. He set up all of my connections there and has helped in huge ways. Ken's first connection with Kenya was helping write a newsletter for Ingili to help gain sponsorships for that school, so it was great to see both the primary and high schools.

Allan was able to say "hi" and share with Ken a little more informa-tion on how to get started on a secondary school. First, get a title deed to the property, not just a bill of sale. Second, get plans drawn up for the school. Then, send the plans and the title deed to the Minister of Education (the cabinet secretary for education) in Nairobi to get their approval for a secondary school. If approved, they will give you a checklist of necessary details.

It was helpful information from someone who had started a high school just one year ago. I also got to say hello to Anne (the amazing matron and chef at our Bomani school). It was great to see her and pass along greetings from people back in the States.

## MY LOVE FOR THE PEOPLE OF TIWI

Then it was off to meet up with Liz at Crossroads Fellowship in Nyali, and to head down to the South Coast. Once on the South Coast, we first met up with Elias, the person who runs the Lutheran Orphanage and Primary school. He gave us a tour of both places and again reiterated the need for a high school, even before he knew why we were there. Another God moment. It was such a God thing that the land was already purchased, so it was just a matter of building a few buildings, buying supplies, and getting some sponsors for the high school children.

Elias showed us the property where the orphanage was, and all the extra land around it where the secondary school would go. At first, we were concerned because a lot of the land is very hilly. Although it is beautiful, with palm trees amongst the hills, it would be difficult to build on. However, after walking most of the property, we were able to find a way to lay out a site plan so that only flat areas of the property would be utilized for building.

Then we headed to the hotel to check in. After about two hours of "discussions", we finally got our room at an appropriate rate. It is a very nice place, Diani Reef, and we were very comfortable and well fed. Much better food than the Neptune, where we stay in Mombasa. The Neptune is a great hotel, but the food is nothing to write home about. It is edible, just not great. Here at the Diani Reef, the food is wonderful. I showered, read a book, and headed off to bed to prepare for a huge day tomorrow. It was the first activity day that is 100% my responsibility. I was praying it would go well.

We started the day in a planning session with Issac, Fred, and Pastor Vincent. Pastor Vincent is one of Tiwi's founders, an amazing man of courage and honor for God. From there we went to the baby class and gave each of the children a hat, then left them some toys to play with for the day. It was so cute to see the tables full of tiaras and construction hats.

Next we did a short visit to the kindergarten classes.

After that we went to our biggest project of the day -- running four activity stations for the lower elementary age kids, with only three adults.

**STATION ONE:** Basketballs donated from the YMCA, and a few soccer balls from outside donations. The kids don't get exposed to many other sports other than soccer. It was fun to teach them basketball. Ken was in charge of that, as well as another outside station,

**STATION TWO:** Jacks and basketball. One end of the court was a shooting hoop for basketball, and the other side was for Jacks.

**STATION THREE:** Art station. The kids used crayons and finger-paints to create artwork. The children had so much fun with that station that they did not want to leave it. Our friend, Liz, manned this station.

**STATION FOUR:** I was handing out the hats that had been donated to every child and then did a short lesson on how hats protect us from the sun and rain, but God protects us even more than a hat, if we believe in Him.

They did so well. We spoke about their favorite subjects in school and what they wanted to be when they grew up. We also talked about other occupations that they never speak of—accountants, journalists, broadcasters. Almost every one of them wanted to be a doctor, pilot, or lawyer.

Tiwi is my favorite place. It was where I fell in love with Kenya for the first time. Tiwi and the South Coast are very dark places. Not literally, but spiritually and culturally. For the most part, the only religion, if any, is Islam. I don't see a lot of churches or mosques in this part of Kenya. However, even bigger than that I think, is the tribalism/witchcraft that is rampant here, and the people are extremely loyal to their tribes. They will fight physically, legally, and any other way you can think of to keep someone of another tribe down, even if it means they go down with them.

Most of South Coast is filled with the Diego people who are traditionally Muslim, though very few seem to practice their religion. Tiwi was the first school Operation Give Hope built. We went to the Diego community because it was a group of people who were at that point unreached by the Gospel. South Coast probably still has some areas that are unreached. The kids are just about the only way to reach the parents and even then the parents are resistant. Our new medical clinic in Tiwi has helped reach out to more people with the Gospel on South Coast.

I took an all heads down, no peeking, raise your hand if you believe in Jesus, secret poll. I would say that close to half of the kids admitted to believing in Jesus, more in the upper grades than the lower ones which is totally understandable, as they are still too young to grasp the concept.

Next, Ken and I did the hat/protection Bible study with all the upper primary kids and gave them their hats. We also did a career education time for these older kids and talked about how to figure out what career they might want to pursue. We talked to them about our careers as teachers, salesmen, and lawyers. We listed a lot of different career possibilities, and how those careers might relate to certain subjects in school. At the end we had them raise their hand to tell us what they wanted to be when they grew up.

We broke them into groups based on their chosen careers. We had groups for teachers, doctors (two groups), pilots, lawyers, pastors, Kenyan Army soliders, and engineers. Each group had a worksheet to fill out about their career, what education was needed, where they would work, and what subjects they would need to study that fit their career choices. It was very interesting how many of them underestimated the amount of schooling for most of the careers, though some of the groups were right on track.

To wrap everything up, Liz and I asked them all to become journalists for Operation Give Hope, as we needed articles about their stories to share. They should write what the school meant to them, or how Jesus had changed their lives. I hoped they followed through on that, especially the older kids.

## SOUTH COAST DAY TWO

We started early in the morning for Tumaini, the Operation Give Hope preschool. It is quite a long drive. Once we got there, we saw first hand the tough times the school was going through. Rain had been hitting the area hard. We still had two mud classrooms on this property that housed all the kids for their studies. One full school classroom and one wall of another had been totally washed away by the rain and winds. Additionally, Pastor Stephen was being harassed by local authorities, saying that if he didn't pay a certain amount of money, they would take his benches, which was just about all the school had left.

It was heartbreaking to see and hear this. The amount of funds necessary to rectify this problem fully was probably less than $50. The problem was if we took $50 to rectify it from our current funds available, it would be $50 less to feed kids with. This situation again shows how such a small amount can make such a huge difference in the lives of kids, teachers, and pastors in Kenya. This is one area where having extra funds in our general account would help out immensely.

We greeted each classroom and they sang us some songs and presented us with some homemade crosses the kids made out of sticks. We also had a chance to see the community pond that was still being used for drinking water, even though there was a clean well provided by Operation Give Hope. Remember, this is the place with the pond that has crocodiles in it and is very dirty from sewer run off. The villagers say the well water is too salty so they continue to fetch water from the pond instead. The well water is fine to our tastebuds. We had the well tested, and all the levels are appropriate. But the people around Tumaini are used to dirty water and they don't like the taste of the clean well water.

This is a prime example of why community education is so important when bringing in projects like the well. Through our medical teams and other efforts of the church and school, we are providing education.

However, it could have been done earlier, before the well project started. The community should have been more involved in the project from beginning to end.

On the way out of town, we headed back to Tiwi for 30 minutes to take a few more photos. Then, it was time for the ferry back over to Mombasa. It is always so hard to leave. The staff are amazing.

After the ferry, we made our first stop at the purse store in Shanzu. I had a large order from a church in upper Michigan, thanks to my amazing dear friend, Barb Gabriel. I also have a few orders from some of my other friends back home. The shop was pretty empty, though, and they had totally changed the items they carried, so orders would be difficult in the future. However, I did find out that I could email them ahead of time with colors and items, and they would make them to order. This would make things much easier. They also provide shipping, but at additional cost, which would cut into the little profit that came from each item sold. All the profits go towards land to build the adoption resource center.

By 3:00 pm, it was back to the hotel in northern Mombasa to shower and hunt down my Kenyan phone. I finally found my phone and got it working, but not until close to 6:00 pm. I was also not able to get a meeting with Vicky and Hellen, the Kenyan lawyer and psychologist we were working with on the adoption center in 2012.

However, I was able to steal Pastor Allan, the busiest man in Kenya, to take me to view property for the adoption resource center. I was so excited about this. The property was literally right off the road, and in a great location.

By morning, I was expecting the arrival of the rest of the group from Fox River Church, but their plane had been delayed, and then the group was rerouted around the world. They finally arrived while we were eating dinner, about 7:30pm. Their arrival was not without a lot of travel nightmares, and of course, lost luggage.

I could see now that this trip was going to be different than any other Fox River trip before in more ways than one.

*Chapter 3*

# A Trip Like No Other – Keeping the Right Attitude

## June 2012: Whole Fox River Team, Pam

The rest of the group arrived safely and we were grateful for that. Unfortunately, the only bag that they brought with them was the bag that I had lost days before. All the rest of the luggage, except for a piece or two, was lost by the airlines in the 12 hour flight delay rerouted around the world drama. Not only were the clothes and all personal items lost, but also all the activities we were going to do with the kids. All these things come with us in our bags, so no luggage meant a lot of last minute changes for what the trip would entail and how it would proceed.

### ATTITUDE IS THE MOST IMPORTANT PART

There were some struggles on the trip for me and I was really angry about a few things that had happened. They affected the very limited time I had to meet with my partners, Vicky and Hellen, to continue our adoptions work. Due to some, what I felt were self-centered choices of others, I was unable to contact Vicky and Hellen until Tuesday evening at 6:00 pm. By this time it was too late to meet. They were no longer available. We had been spending marathon days in the centers and not getting back until really late, so we had not been able to meet during the week either. Additionally, Vicky was going to be out of town for the weekend. I had been there for over a week at this point and had been unable to connect with them at all.

Not being able to meet with Vicky and Hellen was a really difficult thing for me to move past. I was murmuring and complaining to myself in my thoughts, to my roommate Pam, and to Ken. Luckily, Pam called me on it and said, "You're just going to have to let it go or you will stay stuck there," and, "There is no way to change it." I had a choice: spend time complaining about people and/or situations that I couldn't change or focus on God and do what He wanted me to do.

Murmuring and complaining is something we do in our culture and no one calls us on it. It is not a good practice in any situation. It does not fix problems and it keeps you stuck on them. God has a lot to say in the Bible about murmuring and complaining, and it is not positive. It's something I work hard at everyday and I'm grateful for people like Pam for calling me on it.

Once I stopped complaining, God was able to show me He had things under control. He had some other people He wanted me to meet that would help get our work accomplished a lot quicker and easier.

My friend Penninah came to visit one night. We spoke about the adoption work that was going forward and she wanted to help in any way she could. She would be going to Eygpt in August and would be taking African jewelry to sell there for the project. She also came up with a few ideas as possibilities with the church there in Kenya.

I also had some deep discussions with my friend Jayne Claire on what God was showing her. She felt directed to write, to help fundraise for non-profits, and she felt called to create a Pregnancy Crisis Center.

Joy, the amazing massage and nail technician, discussed her interest in helping with the mission of adoption, and possibly adopting herself, at some point in the future. Pam and I got our nails done, too, which is always a treat. If you make it to Kenya, do not leave without some service from Joy. She is skilled in reflexology, massage, and nails. She is amazing.

## SHOES

After the few people that had clothes shared with those who did not, we were on our way to the first activity for the trip. We went to Kreme Primary School in Bomani, the free school. Fox River was able to get enough shoes purchased through the church to fit the whole school of 1500 kids with shoes. That is an incredible number of shoes! 1500 more children are able to walk with their feet covered to avoid disease, which can lead to infection and death, thanks to people donating $5 per pair for the shoes. The cost of the shoes is even less than that per pair, but includes shipping and a few other expenses. After we distributed the shoes at the school, we still had enough left over to take into the community to hand them out there as well.

We took a photo of all the students at the school by the flagpole holding up their shoes. It was very humbling to see how excited they were for something so simple, and how it may very well be the best thing they would receive all year, or ever. It's amazing to think that people around the world made this happen for them, with very little sacrifice.

Every year we also leave the school with a few desks and school supplies. It is great to see how much better the free school is getting year after year. It seems like only the little ones are sitting on the ground for class now, as today almost everyone has a desk. The students are still really crowded, but at least they are on desks and not on the dirt floor.

## MUSIC

Music is such a huge part of the African culture. Instruments are not necessary. People will use their feet, hands, clothing, and voices to make the beat and rhythm. One class at the free school recited a poem for us on education. They also sang a song for us about that day being the best day of their lives. The childrens' voices are so amazing, and they never have music in the background. They do so amazingly well it brings me to tears. Every time we come, the classes share their music with us. This year, we did something new; we presented a song we learned in Swahili to the kids at Bomani and Vipingo that talked about looking and searching for God. They were so shocked that we could sing the song in Swahili that some of them looked like they were going to cry. They were so honored that we would sing to them in their language.

## SCHOOLS, KIDS, AND TEACHERS

Next, we headed off to New Life School in Bomani, Kenya. This is one of the schools completely supported by Fox River Christian Church in Waukesha, Wisconsin. They support the school, church, well, and feeding center. It is just down the street from the free school in Bomani. The kids were so excited to see us that they, too, sang to us into their compound. We listened to their songs and poems, and then we fed them lunch.

We had a lot of fun getting to know Martha and Francis, two teachers at Bomani, a little better. We did a few different team building games with them, and they took us to their classrooms and told us how they run their rooms and classes. It was very interesting to learn more about it and to find out that their grades are very similar to our grades. Some of the teachers, but not all of them, have a home on the property of the school. We felt privileged to get a chance to see the homes that are on the property. It's humbling. They have single rooms to live in, with one single bed each. Some of the teachers have two children that live with them. It's a different reality, and it shows us the difference between "need" and "want."

I was also able to find Alfred and Mariam, kids I met the first time I came to Kenya in 2008, with whom I have reconnected every time I come back. We got a few pictures and said hello. Nevvy also found me. Nevvy was a little boy Josie fell in love with last year on the trip. He was expecting to see her and was disappointed when she wasn't there. It turns out that Nevvy is Mariam's brother, which I did not know.

## THINGS SEEM TO BE COMING TOGETHER

While we were all serving lunch at Bomani, I got a chance to talk with a missionary, Lisa Bechtel, a great woman who has three amazing stories of adoption with their three boys, one international and two from the U.S. She and her husband are very interested in opening an adoption center and orphanage in Kenya.

I also finally had a chance to have a great conversation with Jim Horne, the missionary I've been working with for Operation Give Hope. I gave him more details about the plans to go ahead with an adoption resource center.

He was supportive, and indicated if we could get a big enough plot of land, he would handle the construction of a church, a day care school, and a feeding center on the property. We would also include an Operation Give Hope office. He gave advice and suggestions on how to proceed. I now needed to talk with Alan to see how large of a plot he would sell. Jim was drawing up the plans for me for the layout and other things, and I was working on raising the funds -- at least $50,000 -- for the 1/2 acre of land that was needed.

## COMMUNITY VISIT

Next, our group went out into the community to see the homes and how the people live in Kenya. The homes are the hardest part for the group. The people in these communities are so thankful for what they have, yet we are used to something so different. Their reality is mud-huts, or possibly cement blocks, if they are very lucky.

We spent some time in the poorest area of the Vipingo community. In most of Vipingo, Kenyans live in one room mud huts. Well-off families sleep in one bed, usually without a mattress, just mosquito netting. They have no possessions, maybe one extra set of clothes for a child, if they are really well off.

Our reality is so different. We take so much for granted. We don't even realize how most people in the rest of the world live.

We were in Vipingo to deliver shoes and mosquito nets to as many people as we could. Guys enrolled at the Bible college came with us and we all shared the Gospel while we shared the love of God's caring hands.

Close to 10 people came to Christ through this outreach. It's amazing how much faster people accept Christ here. In the US and other developed areas, we have so many other options. We can buy a bigger house, get a better car, buy a boat, get an education, take that weekend empowerment course, watch certain TV shows, read the perfect book, or do whatever else we convince ourselves will make our lives have more meaning. In other countries, people don't have all these options, and because of that, choices are so much simpler and life has so much more meaning. This is an example of how our wealth can be such a huge hindrance to us, and we don't even realize it.

## ORPHANAGE VISIT

I went back to visit Good Life Orphanage, the one that was run like a foster care system with kids of all different ages living under one roof with a mom and an auntie. The orphanage does everything in a small house, which is awesome. I was connected with a friend of mine, Jenna, who was interested in looking into starting an orphanage in Kenya shortly after my last trip. The Good Life Orphanage was the one place I wanted to show her as a great example to follow in her work. Through the trip that summer, she realized God wanted her to slow down a little. She wanted to move to Kenya immediately to work on this project with some local missionaries, but in prayer, she realized that God wanted her to work on her education first. She will be hard at work on that over the next few years. Good luck, Jenna, and way to follow God even when it's not what you want to do.

As a result of rain delay in getting back to Vipingo, the whole group had several hours to talk with George, the social worker at Good Life. We asked him so many questions about orphanages, regulations, adoption, and life in general. He told us about Father Dolan, from Ireland, also a lawyer, doing somewhat similar work with the police department, targeting police brutality and torture issues. He set up a meeting with him for me later in the week.

## RELAXING

I woke up at 5:00 am, but didn't get out of bed until 8:15 am. Pam and I headed straight down to the ocean, Pam with her journal, and I with my morning readings. It was such a relaxing time and place. The Indian Ocean is beautiful. High tide brings the sound of the waves so much closer, and it keeps the people that sell curios on the beach out of sight which makes it much more enjoyable.

We ate breakfast with the quieter part of the group, which was nice. It was off to church at Crossroads Nyali after that. It's a church just like our church, Fox River, in the states. Contemporary, but Fox River is at least 10 times louder with their music, so it's not your "normal church". It was great to see lots and lots of people I knew, and it was also great to recharge. I knew I needed some quality quiet time with God so I stayed back Sunday from Bomani so I could reconnect and recharge.

## SPECIAL TIME TO WORK - HARSH REALITIES

While the rest of the group went on safari, I was able to stay back and work on other things for our project. Dorcas Blessing and Jayne Claire came around with me for the day. We revisited all the orphanages from our last visit. We saw Peter and Selpher Mutua in their Baby Life Rescue Center, Tammi and Patrick at Upiende Orphange, and Wana Wa Mola's Boys Home.

We went back to Violet's school, New Hope. We visited with all the girls and encouraged them to stay in school and stay focused on their dreams. We had a panel discussion with three Kenyans and myself. We talked to the girls about sticking to their dreams and staying in school by sharing our stories.

We also had a question and answer session. This is when I was hit with another harsh reality of life in Kenya, especially life in the slums of Kenya very near the coast. We had quite a few questions from the girls about what to do when guys come up to them and want them to go "work" at the beach. They promise them big paychecks which they can bring back and support their families with.

The truth is that these guys want them to become sex-slaves to tourists. They will get little, if any, funds and may not ever be returned to their homes. These girls need to run to avoid these contacts. The men are sitting there waiting to prey on them as they walk home from school. The reality is, in Kenya, households have very little, if any, income coming in. They have no food pantries to turn to, and there is no government assistance of any kind. At times this appears to be a good option for them, especially when they are literally starving. It is a harsh, sad reality for girls in many parts of the world.

When I sit at home and think about orphans, sex trafficking, world hunger, it is very easy to wish it was different, not really knowing what to do, and therefore do nothing. It is much harder to do nothing when you hear an eleven-year-old girl pleading with you for help right in front of your face.

But the truth is, whether I am sitting at home in New Berlin, Wisconsin, or I am seeing it face-to-face in Mombasa, Kenya, these things are happening. Every day, every minute. And the reality is we can do something. Maybe it is coming to a place to help face-to-face. Maybe it is researching to find an organization to donate to that is doing great work like us. Or maybe it is organizing an event to create awareness and raise funds for an organization. Whatever it is, I hope we all say a prayer and do something to help these girls and boys today.

## DAY TWO OF SPECIAL PROJECTS

We spent the second day with George, the social worker from Good Life Orphanage. He took us all around downtown to the Children's Department in Mombasa. The line was very long and the employee we needed to see was late. The area the adoption resource center would be in was Mtwapa, which was in the Kiliffii district, so we left without seeing anyone. However, I did see the sign that was supposed to have been changed to "Pilgrim's Adoption Resource Center". It had not been changed, which is alarming to me because I had been sending over several hundred dollars a month to support this venture, only to find out the sign had not been changed.

Next, we headed to Children's Court in Tonoko. Unfortunately, it was not in session. The courthouse consisted of an open air pavilion. While we were there, we found the CRADLE office. CRADLE is a UNICEF funded organization that takes woman's cases to court for child support and other woman related issues. Faith was great, and got us in touch with a man by the name of Collins, who was the head lawyer for that location at that time. He was very helpful in giving us information about the process and where he saw needs in the system. We were not able to meet with him in person but were able to speak by phone and email.

We then headed out to Kiliffii to visit the Children's Department, which is the district where the property for the orphanage is located. It was my first visit that far north and was in a small rural village. We were at the Children's Department to ask for a checklist on the steps to follow to open an adoption agency. The director did not have any answers to our questions, but assured us she would get them that day or the next.

After Kiliffii, we dropped George off in Mtwapa and headed to Shanzu for the Girl Guide purses. The order was not ready, so Jayne, Dorcus, and I sat outside and talked through the plans for a run/walk, which was awesome.

Back at the hotel, Father Dolan came to visit. Father Dolan has been in Kenya since, I believe, the 1970's. He was originally a lawyer from Ireland, and has done a lot of landlord, tenant, and other legal work for people in the slums around Mombasa. After hearing about the adoption work we were doing, he strongly encouraged us to work in the area of a pregnancy crisis center. He indicated the only option for women in Mombasa, who are pregnant, is to call Maristops for help. He explained that Maristops is simply a front for people to call to and get a referral to a place for an abortion. He indicated that it was a great need. It was wonderful to talk with him and hear about what he was doing, and get guidance from him for our project.

## WHY INTERNATIONAL MISSIONS?

One of the biggest moments for me personally occurred while we were driving away from the Bomani free school. We had our boxed lunches from the hotel with us that we were to give to people in the village as we drove by. We each got a box and could choose who to give it to. We remained on the bus at all times, so it was only a brief moment that we got to connect with them. Watching everyone hand their boxes out, you could see children and families so excited and grateful for the food. A little boy ran home to show his mom what he got in the box lunch. So many others were running, yelling and were so very grateful.

Our bus pulled alongside a woman in the village. She had a few children tagging along with her, and one on her back as well. She was walking, so she had no idea what we were doing. When we pulled alongside, I opened my window and handed my lunch box to the woman. As she took it into her hands and took a quick peek at what was inside, she started crying. The eyes of the little girl alongside her started dancing. As we pulled away, you could hear screaming, "Asante, asante, asante," (thank you, thank you, thank you) and then, "karibu, karibu, karibu" (welcome, welcome, welcome). The moment brought me to tears. So grateful for a banana, a roll, and a hard-boiled egg. With so many children for her to feed, they each would only get a bite or two, yet she showed such extreme gratitude. The sad reality was that once that food was gone, she and her children would be starving again.

I was grateful to be of some help, but there is so much more to be done. We can solve this problem, but everyone needs to do their part. In international missions, a little bit of money goes a long way. For example, through Operation Give Hope, $5 per month can feed a child two meals a day every school day. Five dollars per month. 40 meals. Meals, which mean the difference between life and death.

Another example of a little bit of money making a huge difference is happening in Bomani. You may remember the women in Bomani from the March 2012 trip with Sue Huerta, when we did the Bible study with them for the first time. They were very distant, very quiet. In fact, they didn't speak at all. There was no hope in them or seemingly around them. We left after hearing questions like, "How can we get our children to behave better?" Answering with, "Make sure they get enough rest." Their response back is, "They rock back and forth all night unable to sleep because they are starving!"

To say that conversation left a mark on my psyche would be putting it mildly. We have no idea what people in the rest of the world have to deal with. At least I didn't have any real idea. Sue and I both knew we had to do something. We didn't know what exactly, but through prayer and conversation, we pulled an idea together.

We could address the spiritual point of view easily by implementing a women's Bible study. Obviously that was not the only need they had. So, when we got home, we went to work. We were able to find the funds to get the ladies started in a jewelry making business. They will be trained in making jewelry. They will come together as a community to make the jewelry that will help them pool their resources, even at the beginning of the project before funds come in. Along with the project, the ladies will attend a Bible study together every week.

Not to give away the ending, but as a foreshadowing - you will not believe what I saw when I returned just a handful of months later! More to come! We can all make a huge difference with very little sacrifice, but are we willing?

## PIECES OF THE PUZZLE

When I speak at different events, one of the activities we sometimes do has a very deep meaning. I hand everyone in the audience one piece of a jigsaw puzzle. Imagine you have one puzzle piece you are holding in your hand. Remember back to a time when you have done a jigsaw puzzle. Maybe it was one of a gorgeous sunset, fall trees, or a winter scene.

Remember when you did the puzzle that you may have picked up at a rummage sale or at the Goodwill? You worked for hours, or maybe even days, on that puzzle, and you were coming in for a landing and ready to finish it off. Only a few pieces left, and then you realize it -- there is a piece missing. All that work. All that time. All that effort. All of that, for what? A piece is missing. It ruins the whole puzzle-making experience. It feels like a complete waste. Just one missing piece makes those other 999 pieces feel meaningless.

In God's plan, all of our lives are one piece of a great big puzzle. We all have our one "piece" to share. We bring our puzzle "piece" to this world. If we choose to wait or ignore or not do our part, the puzzle will feel like it wasn't worth it for some people, it will not all fit together. We all have to stand up and include our "piece" of the puzzle.

I hope you have been or will begin journaling and praying about what that piece is for you. We all have one, and it is outside your home. We all have mission work to do inside our homes with our spouses and our kids, that is one part of our mission work, but God also calls us to help outside of that arena. We need to push in, be willing to listen, and then get to work doing what we hear, even if it doesn't seem to make sense to us.

## CARRYING TOO MUCH BAGGAGE

Almost 10 days later, we headed to the airport with some of our travelers still without their bags. Though lack of luggage was very difficult for the team, no one complained about it at all, and it taught us a few important lessons.

First, it taught us flexibility. The supply suitcases were not there in time for our activity days with the kids, so we had to move the activities to later in the trip. We did other activities early. After the trip was over, it was obvious to all travelers who had been to Kenya before that doing the activity days last was a better way to run the trip. God used the luggage problems to teach us a lesson. Be flexible, because the way we think things should be planned is not necessarily the best way.

Second, the missing luggage brought us back to the real purpose of the trip. The trip had started to become a little too focused on what we were bringing or doing, and not on developing relationships. What we were actually supposed to be bringing was a time of hope and love. Without our bags, hope and love is all we had to offer, and it brought us all back to the real reason for these trips – people, not things.

The third lesson was a reminder that we all survived with very little "stuff". The suitcase we packed full of clothes and other items? Well, we lived without most of it for over a week, a lesson that we pack too heavy. This is not only true of our suitcases, this is also true of our lives.

We carry things around with us that are better left off. We carry around negative emotions, unwillingness to forgive, time pressures, perfectionism, and so much more. It does nothing to help us, and it makes things so much more difficult. Yet we choose to carry these things around with us every day.

Let's start today and make a conscious effort to not carry these things around anymore. Let's forgive the person who did the unthinkable to you. Forgive not for them, but for you. They aren't thinking about what they did every day and wasting their life over it. You are and, as a result, are wasting your life.

Let go of perfectionism. Let's start rolling with the punches of life just for what they are, and not for what we want them to be. Life will be so much more productive, worthwhile, and joyful. Give it some thought. Take some time to journal. What do you need to "unpack" from your emotional suitcase of stuff?

## MEMORABLE MOMENTS

During my quiet times on this trip, I was reflecting on my trips to Kenya and thinking, we all have our own personal "Kenya". Those places where God is calling us to make a difference, in our neighborhood, in our church, in our family, in our state, and in our world.

We need to make sure we are following that lead and doing what God is calling us to do. Not finding excuses, not leaving it for tomorrow or a more convenient time. When we do that, people are left suffering, waiting for us, or the next person God calls, to help them.

Although this book, for the most part, simply outlines the work happening in Kenya, God leads me to a lot of work here in the States as well -- helping a pregnant mom get the things together she needs to have a baby, giving legal advice to someone served with divorce papers who cannot afford a lawyer, driving my kids to and fro, and many other things.

Whatever and whoever God puts in my path, those are the people God is calling me to reach. I need to be open to seeing this, and open to help, even if it is not convenient, easy, or in my time frame. I hope you are making it a priority to find your "Kenya" and are pursuing it.

Whatever God puts in front of you, do it. Do it promptly and see where it leads you. I can tell you from experience - you will be amazed!

## UNEXPECTED MISSION CHANGING MOMENT

It is now the last day of the trip and I finally get to meet with Vicky for the first time on the adoption center work. Hellen is unavailable. Jayne Claire also joined us for the meeting. It started out as a really good meeting. We talked about how we needed to get refocused on our goals. We easily came to an agreement on what those goals were, as we had outlined them in our earlier meetings. They were easy to come back to and refocus on. I tended to follow Hellen and Vicky's lead. If I had thoughts, I would put them in to be weighed, but I didn't hang tight to my thoughts and ideas, because I was not in my culture. Kenyans know Kenyan culture better than anyone.

It felt like we had really recharged and come to an understanding and agreement on what would happen, and in what order. In the middle of the meeting, the delivery of the Shanzu bags arrived. I quickly ran upstairs to grab the money to pay for the bags, paid, and sat back down in my chair.

At that point, Vicky started saying over and over again that I had all the answers. I told her, "I don't have all the answers, Vicky, we all are coming together to figure out where this is all going." She just kept repeating that I had all the answers, then promptly grabbed her stuff, and left.

I was shocked. I had no idea what had just happened. We had such a productive meeting and we were moving along so well without any arguments. I had no idea where this had come from or what it meant.

That was it! It was all done. All these years of work, numerous trips and countless hours, all gone in the blink of an eye.

## HEADING HOME

As I left Kenya in June, 2012, I was very hurt and confused. I felt like I was free-falling. Had this all been a waste of time, money, and energy? What happened with Vicky so suddenly? Why was this happening? What was happening? I was dazed and confused. Did this mean the end of God's work for me in Kenya?

*Chapter 4*

# Rejection Is Hard to Take

Now I was home, and wasn't confused for long on where things stood with Vicky and Hellen after the crazy meeting. Before I even got home there was an email in my inbox from Hellen's office. She asked me for my resignation from PARC so she could continue the work solo. So I sent my resignation the same way that Vicky had asked for it, through an email. However, her office indicated that an email was not enough; I needed to do more. It was a month of drama, back and forth. At this point, my feelings were that I wanted to be done with Kenya. I was rejected, hurt, and still very confused at what caused this.

## WRITING

At the same time, through a variety of leadings all year long, I now had confirmation that I was to write a book. The topic of the book was to be Kenya. At the beginning of the year, I knew God was leading me to write more. I'm not a writer. In fact, I hated English in school. The thought was very overwhelming, but again, same as the half marathon running we talked about in the last book, I broke it down into steps and started one word at a time to see where it led.

I started by attending two writers' groups. First, there was the Milwaukee's Writers Workshop, where I attended a seminar/class on short-story writing. It was the only class that they had available right away, so I jumped right in. Second, I attended the writer's workshop at Hales Corners Lutheran Church, which was free. They met the first and third Saturdays of the month at 8:45-10:30ish, and were very informal. People would simply share their writings and then ask for feedback.

Through the workshops, I got my hands on a book by Rochelle Melander, *Write-A-Thon: Write Your Book in 26 Days (and Live to Tell About It)*. It seemed to fit perfectly with my two-large goals that year; writing and running. The book made comparisons throughout about writing a book being the same as training for a marathon. I read the 170ish page book that first Saturday of January. Ideas were flowing. Everything from deciding on a topic, to how to research, and so much more.

The book was a great read and very inspiring, but at that point, it left me more confused on what topic God was calling me to write about. Given a situation that happened the year before with someone I worked with in high school, I thought I was being called to write about what it takes for a teen to recover after sexual assault, but I was not sure.

I was confused, but I kept going through the entire 12-week short story class. Through the Hales Corners Writers Workshop I got a lot of leads about other one-day seminars and writing workshops, so I signed up for a few of those. However, I still didn't know the topic to write about.

After the March 2012 trip to Kenya, I randomly forwarded my blog to the leader of the Hales Corners group for him to read through. It was very long. He read the whole thing within one day and indicated I should turn it into a book. That was around April, but I still didn't feel Kenya was the "right" first book. I felt the sexual assault book would help more people, and be more useful to others, so I continued working on it.

After returning from the most recent trip to Kenya, and all the rejection and uncertainty surrounding it, I knew it was God's second sign that Kenya was the way to go for the first book. Again, having no idea how this process works, I just took those steps I knew how to take one step at a time. After that, the rest of the steps just revealed themselves.

First, I started reworking the blog. Blog writing is much different than book writing. I printed out all the blogs as my starting point, reworked them, and added in a little more emotion to my earlier writing. I also had to write the back story of how I ended up in Kenya in the first place, which hadn't been in the blog.

I am always learning, and the way we learn is to take the first, and then next step, one after the other, and see what doors open and where they lead. We don't know all the answers. We never will, but we have to start somewhere.

What do you need to start today that you have been putting off for years? Just take the first step today and see what happens.

### I COULDN'T DO IT WITHOUT THE SUPPORT OF OTHERS

Without the dedicated support of my friend, Pat Molitor, I don't know if I would have had the courage to take the first steps. I was very hesitant, resistant and scared to have anyone else read my work. I do not like grammar. I was embarrassed to send my first draft to anyone I didn't know personally. I thought all writers know grammar rules, all of them, so I was very unsure of myself on those things. Since then, I have realized that it is actually the editor who knows those rules much better than authors. At the time, I would not have taken the first step without Pat to do my initial edit.

I have another friend who does work on a website called Elance.com. Elance is a website for just about any profession or occupation, from lawyers, to editors, graphic artists, web designers, and many more. It's a place where people post jobs they need completed, and people with those skill sets can bid on the jobs to do the work. Elance is a spin-off of the term freelance.

Anyway, at some point in the classes I was taking, I knew I needed to find at least two editors, and a graphic artist for the cover and other page layout work. I had priced it out and was going at it in the cheapest way possible. It would cost around $4,000 to get all this work done! I had no idea where that money was going to come from. I was funding the project myself, but I just kept moving forward and let God take care of the bill.

So I went about posting advertisements for the various jobs that needed to be done for the book. Bids were coming in, and I had no idea how to decide which person to choose. On Elance, you get a bio of the person with examples of their previous work, and they write to you and tell you what they will do and for how much. This is great information to go through if you have just a few people bidding, but I had over fifty bids!

It was overwhelming, and remember, I was writing the book at the same time as I was getting these things lined up. Luckily, my friend, Ara Jackson, who does work on Elance, was able to help me weed through a lot of bids and narrow them down to three. After corresponding with those three, one person rose way above the others; Penny Swift.

Penny Swift is from South Africa. She saw the project and the mission work it was going to support, which prompted her initial interest. She gave me so much information and guidance, even in the initial bid, way before any commitment to work together. She was so helpful.

The world of publishing is very foreign to me. Penny was so patient with all my seemingly irrelevant questions and so many other details that she had to walk me through by hand. Penny had edited and graphically laid out a great many books before this one. She was a Godsend, and she was willing to do all the work involved for just $250. I was previously expecting the work to cost about $4,000. I am still in awe of all she has taught me, and the fact that she was willing to help us with the cause for well below her normal rate. Thank you, Penny Swift! Without you, that book would not have been possible.

## WRITING - WE ALL SHOULD WRITE

Not all of us write to be published. Many of us write for our family and friends so they can read our story. Some of us write in a journal to be closer to God. Still others of us write to work through our own emotions. Whatever you write, and whatever your reasons are, I encourage you to keep it up, and be deliberate about it. If you don't write, I would strongly encourage you to start.

Writing brings so much clarity to confusing situations. It brings renewed purpose and encouragement. I truly believe God has called us all to share our stories. We do it in person, which is great, but we can also do it through writing. Our writings will last long after we have passed on.

Write thank you/encouragement notes, write a blog, write a journal, write Facebook posts that make a difference, type out emails that bring people up, or write a book. Whatever it is, take a leap of faith. Even if you don't "like" to write, do a little everyday. It will make a huge difference in your own life, and possibly someone else's life, too.

In July, 2012, I spent one week writing the first book in this now-series! I would actually say that God wrote the book. The whole week was really a blur. As I was writing, I was emailing with Elance people, and then Penny.

She had the cover done by Wednesday and I didn't even "hire" her till Monday. The whole process was so smooth. At the same time, I had three previously scheduled writing classes that I attended that week. In addition to the writing, there is a lot of marketing that needs to be done for books, so I was working various bio sheets for writing and speaking engagements. I was also doing all the administrative parts of book writing: obtaining ISBN numbers, Amazon CreatesSpace accounts, etc. It was certainly a whirlwind week, but every minute was worth it!

When I met with people after they had read the book, they would bring up a certain part that they particularly enjoyed or related to. Many of the times, I didn't even remember that the part they were referring to was in the book! To write this book, I had to read the first book to make sure I wasn't repeating myself, or some of the stories I had told. God truly did write the book through me. It was not of my own energy or thoughts; it was through Him.

Putting your life out there for people to see and read provides a lot of chances for the devil to pull you down. Given that, the project brought many spiritual attacks. I was going through a lot of rejection by friends at the time, and then the thought of putting the book out there for even more rejection was a bit overwhelming. Thanks to the encouragement of my dear friend Pat Molitor, I was able to work through it and continue on God's journey for me. The devil had my attention focused on the wrong things, on all the negative. Thank you, Pat, for redirecting my thoughts.

At the same time, I was getting tremendous support from my husband and family. They took up regular tasks for me so I could focus on writing 15 hours a day for a week and a half in order to get the project completed as soon as possible and into the hands of people who were doing the finishing work. People God led me to work with online helped me with publishing and marketing the project. Kenyans contributed their personal stories, and the stories of the people and children they work with for the "Remember Me" chapter of the book. Pat spent hours and hours doing an initial edit for me so I wasn't embarrassed to send it to my publishing editor. My friend Michelle, and "second mom", Susie, read through the "final draft" once the editor and I were both done with it for one final look-through. Not to mention the organizations, friends, and family that came through financially to help get the book off the ground and into people's hands. Thank you so much for believing in the project even when I did not, and contributing to it in all the ways you did!

The book was a tremendous growing experience for me on so many levels. First, the personal level of working through the above issues of rejection and seeing the positives, and letting my perceived weaknesses shine. I never thought of myself as a good writer, so to put myself out there for anyone to read, including an editor or anyone else, was very difficult.

Second, it was great to look back over all the experiences I had had in Kenya to make sure I was still following God's lead for my work, and not the lead of the others I may have been working with. The possible separation in my relationship with the Kenyan lawyer and psychologist really helped me to let go of the whole situation so I could look at it from God's perspective and make sure I was still on His path. For the most part I was, but there were a few areas I was ignoring that I knew God wanted me to focus on—specifically the pregnancy crises side of things—so the separation and the writing of the book really allowed God to come in and shine a light on where I was to be working.

Writing helps clarify life. Take some time today to write!

## FUND RAISING

No matter what work I would be doing in Kenya, if any at all, funds were needed for the schools and orphanages of Operation Give Hope. Therefore, I spent the summer months working on a few fundraising projects.

The book just was one effort. 100% of the profits went to, and still go towards, the mission work.

## RUN/WALK YEARS IN THE MAKING

In June, we started working on the plan for our first annual "Run/Walk for African Orphans" on Milwaukee's Lakefront. I knew for over a year that God was leading us to organize a run/walk event, but I had no idea what that entailed. God led me through it one step at a time.

The hardest part of planning was setting a date. Should we do summer, spring, or fall? We attempted to do the event in connection with a festival held on our lakefront every year-- African Fest. That event was to take place in August. We met with the coordinator , and it looked like we might be able to come together on it, but time was just not on our side. We had just started this process in mid-June and I was going to be traveling in Kenya for two weeks during that period. Unfortunately, that connection did not work out.

We eventually decided on a date in mid-October. After the book was out of my hands for editing in July, August was spent getting everything set-up and ready for the run. Advertising on Facebook and other places, finding T-shirts, paying for the park, securing insurance, catering etc.

It was a very slow start. One week before the event, I think there were only 15 or so people registered, and most of those were my immediate family and me. A few other close friends, that I knew would not be physically at the event, but just wanted to support it also registered. I was very nervous that no one would be there at all. I was also very afraid that I had spent a ton of money on a park, insurance, T-shirts, food, etc., and that we would not make any money on the event. Remember, all the expenses for a run are up-front costs, so you have to pay for them long before the run takes place. For example, t-shirts and food need to be ordered even if you don't yet have a lot of registrations.

Somehow, God pulled it off without a hitch. We ended up with about 50 people total registered. We covered all of our expenses, which was my goal for the first year, and we made about $750. The event was a great success. Thanks to the amazing volunteers it was easy, effortless, and actually fun! It was cold, but all the volunteers showed up on time and everything went smoothly. It felt like we had just got there and then we were already heading home. We arrived about 6:00 am to start setting up and I was home and doing the accounting work before lunch.

This is an example of how God calls us to do things outside of our comfort zone. I hear people talk of God like He wouldn't ask you to do something that you were not really already good at. That is not my experience at all. God calls us to do things we have no idea how to do. He does this so that He can show us and everyone around us, if we are willing to share it, what amazing things He can do if we just do what He asks, even when we don't know what we are doing.

What is God calling you to do? What is it that you think you have no idea how to go about doing, but you keep being lead towards doing? Take a step today so you can see God work right before your very eyes!

## PEOPLE TO ENCOURAGE YOU

We had two extra special volunteers to help us pull the run/walk event together. Elise, an Alverno student, came alongside and helped with the initial stages of the run/walk. Other current Alverno business students also helped market the event and helped the day of the event. It makes it easier to accomplish something when someone comes with you. Even if they don't do a lot of the work, to have someone to bounce ideas off of and run things by, helps so much.

Sue Huerta has been a constant help and support in that area for me. I am grateful to her for many things. Just being there and being able to talk about life in general, and Kenya, has meant so much to me. There are very few people I will call to vent and truly "yell to" when I am beyond frustrated. She is one of them, and she listens and brings me back to where I need to be.

She is amazing about linking people together and seeing what God does with that. She hosts events, helps plan events, and is always willing to help in whatever way she can. She volunteers to help in many areas and also brings friends along with her. Specifically for the run/walk, she took care of all the route stuff, including the layout, volunteer management, and riding her bike at the front so the run leaders knew where to go next. She also helps with the craft fairs. I am so grateful God has brought her into my life, and into the lives of the Kenyans we work with! Thank you, Sue, for just being you.

## RAISING FUNDS BY SPEAKING ABOUT GOD'S WORKINGS AND KENYA

Another way I saw God leading us in fund raising events was through speaking. I love having the chance to speak about Kenya. I also had the Lutheran Women's Missionary League sponsor the Kenyan Baby Shower in September, 2012. That was so much fun. We learned so much together and we were able to support the children of Kenya.

Sue Huerta hosted a Kenyan baby shower a while later at her Little VIP Preschool and Child Care center. We were hoping to take the "baby shower" presentation on the road and share it with whoever would enjoy this type of event, the story of Kenyan travels, and Operation Give Hope's works. I am also hoping to start speaking more and more. I love sharing the stories of what God has done in my life and is doing in the lives of people all around the world!

## KENYA CRAFTS

As we talked about in the last book, God was calling us to sell crafts to raise funds. It was definitely not the way I would normally go about raising tens of thousands of dollars, but this was what we had.

We started the project at some farmers' markets in the summer. I remember one market right after the 4th of July, when I had just gotten back from Kenya. It must have been 104 degrees in the shade! Elise (the Alverno student) and I were at the farmers' market in South Milwaukee, sweltering away. God didn't say all of this would be easy or comfortable, but I can say it was all worth it. We met some very nice people there. We didn't make a ton of money, but the few that were there were very excited about the crafts we were selling.

One of the best stories that I will ever share came through a farmers' market craft event I was not even present at. Elise was running this one, as I was in Kenya. She relayed the story to me when I returned. She had set everything up and things were going well, similar to the first event - lots of interest but not a ton of sales.

During the evening, a lady approached the table. She showed obvious outward signs of being homeless. She had numerous well worn bags with her, but they were not full of new purchases from the event. Her clothes were dirty and slightly tattered. You could tell she probably lived on the streets.

Sitting at these events by yourself gets lonely and you want to engage people anyway you can to spark up conversation. So Elise shared the story of how the funds we raise from the craft sales go back to Kenya and what

Operation Give Hope is doing in Kenya. Elise then turned to welcome another guest. Later, Elise watched the homeless woman reach in her pocket to pull out some coins and put them in the donation bucket.

As she later relayed the story to me, we were both crying about the whole thing. God will bless those coins more than the rest. It is a reminder of the story in the Bible about the Widow's Offering (Mark 12:41-44, Luke 21:1-4). The wealthy men were putting their large donations into the temple treasury. The poor widow then comes by and donates just two very small coins. Jesus then tells his disciples how her funds were so much more powerful.

How can two small coins be more powerful when they are such a small amount compared to the rich men's large donations? Obviously a large donation will help more than two small coins. But Jesus tells his disciples that her funds were everything she had to live on - not knowing where the next penny would come from. This so very different than the wealthy man who donated a large amount. The rich men did not give everything they had. They gave what was comfortable, and possibly out of obligation. The few small coins are more powerful coming from someone who can afford to give nothing. The poor widow trusted God would take care of her. The rich man trusted his wealth to take care of him.

Well as it turns out, God stayed true to His word! We had a few other small craft fairs at Alverno College in the fall, and a few more at local high schools and nursing homes. In the end we made close to $9,000 between general donations, the run/walk, the craft fairs, and book sales. After the first book was published, I would get random envelopes in the mail with checks and a notes that would say, "after reading your book I had to do something". It was so rewarding and very encouraging.

## RUMMAGES

Every May we host our month-long rummage sale at my mom's house. The rummage sales help pay for trips back and forth to Kenya. I'm not a big fan of rummages. They are a lot of work to set up, but family and friends have been so generous with their donations of items to contribute for the sale. God has blessed those rummages, which usually make around $1,200 per weekend (Thursday, Friday, Saturday)! I can't say no to that. We get a lot of the same customers year after year. It is actually kind of fun to catch up with them. We have been doing these rummage sales since 2008, the first trip to Kenya.

The rummage sale funds are split between whoever works the sale for that weekend, and us. It makes a huge dent in my round trip airfare. Airfare varies greatly, depending on the time of year. Our summer (Kenya's winter) is the most expensive, when I've had to pay in excess of $2,500 for a ticket. The week of New Year's is the best price I've ever found, at $999.87.

Airfare and the price of the driver/van are the two biggest expenses of the trips. Driver expenses are usually around $1,000 per two-week trip with gas, van, driver fees, and tip. The driver fees are divided by the number of people on the trip, which is nice, especially when there are more people going. Thank you to some very generous friends who have also helped to make trips possible for me through donations! So grateful to all who help in every aspect of our work!

## SUPPLY DRIVES MAKE A HUGE DIFFERENCE - TOOTH BRUSHES

Throughout the years we have held various supply drives. We already talked about the baby equipment, but we have also held school supply drives, and requested other specific items that we can take with us over to Kenya.

I once did a Bible study through Hales Corners Lutheran Church called *The Truth Project*. It was an amazing study that talked about how God was visible in everything from science (discussing evolution and other things), to nature, philosophy, and government. If you get the chance, check it out. It was mind boggling. No homework either, just video sessions.

This study took place at my now-friend Cher's house. In the study there were three of us: Cher, Pat Mecha, and I. We had a great run of it for the several weeks we got together. Being such a small class, we really got to know each other quite well. It was during the time of the first run/walk so there were lots of prayers over that event, and other Kenya things. However, Pat surprised me when she said she wanted to do something for the kids in our Kenyan orphanages.

She decided she wanted to bring them toothbrushes, so she started a toothbrush donation drive. Her goal was 500+ toothbrushes. As most drives do, things started out a little bit slow, but she persevered and we ended up with well over the 500+ toothbrush goal.

We couldn't even take all the brushes with us in one trip, there were so many. We had to divide them into two trips. It was really cool to see that effort come together. We took the toothbrushes to all the orphanages and were even able to leave them with several year's supply . We brought so many with us, we were also able to share the toothbrushes with some of the schools we work with.

Dental problems are a big issue in Kenya, so much so that little children's teeth are literally rotting out. Lack of fluoride, access to clean water, and toothbrushes, are a big part of the problem. On the medical mission trips, the most desperate need is for dentists. A lot of the issues they see stem from bad/painful teeth. Various other diseases can start from infected teeth. After reading the posters in the waiting room at my former dentist's office, I know cardiovascular diseases can start from dental problems, so it is very important to deal with these issues before they turn into life threatening medical conditions. It has been very difficult to find dentists willing to commit to going on a trip, dental issues remain a big problem.

Pat is a great example that shows when God puts something on your heart, and you run with it, what He can do can change the world - one brush at a time!

## NEXT TRIP

The tickets were booked in early February 2013 for my ninth trip with Laura Danbrea, a Kenya first-timer, and Sue Huerta, a veteran Kenya missionary. We only had a few months to pull things together. All of us ran separate day care centers in the states, and after some prayer, we thought hosting some "take-out" spaghetti dinners to pay our driver expenses would be a great way to raise much needed funds.

The idea came to me as I was out driving around one day, not really thinking about anything in particular. A take-out spaghetti dinner was not something I had ever thought about before. I love it when God shows Himself like that. Everything goes effortlessly when we follow His lead in those things. I wish I would live in those moments more than I do because they are always there for me. I usually just over-analyze them away.

The spaghetti dinners were a great success. We received rave reviews from many on Facebook, and my day care "babies" even helped me make the desserts!

## PREPARING FOR THE TRIP
## THROUGH THE EYES OF BABIES

It was fun to watch the 1, 2 and 3 year olds in the day care so excited to help. They helped pick out toys for us to take with us to the babies in Kenya. They help us unpack, pack, and so many other things, including stuffing the goodie bags for the run/walk this year.

They were all so excited to see videos and pictures of Kenyan children playing with the toys they had helped pick out. "Show it again, show it again, show it again", they chanted. I will never forget one day, after collecting some of the toys, three-year-old Brody walking into the living room to grab his coat saying, "I have my coat, I'm ready to go to Kenya too!" Then there was the time at lunch when Brody asked what the Kenyan kids got to eat for lunch. I shared a few things that the kids at our schools get, careful to leave out the details of starving children with a three-year-old that was not my child. Brody comes back and says, "I think some of them eat dirt and bugs so their tummies stop hurting because they don't have anything to eat. Do you think that is true?" Three years old and already he realizes all he has to be grateful for, and wants to help and visit those who need more.

I'll also never forget the tireless effort that three-year-old Connor would put in after our school supply drives. We test all the markers to make sure they work before we take them over. Connor is normally a boy of high energy, to say the least! He would sit at the table for HOURS. Long after the other kids went to the other room to play with toys, he was still sitting at the table testing those markers. He was there so long that the other kids would leave and come back to the table to help as he still worked away the whole time. He would not leave the table until every marker was tested. Such commitment and attention span from someone who's normally bouncing off the walls, was definitely a sign of God working through him!

There are so many stories from so many kids that I couldn't even start to list them all. However, I can say I truly look forward to seeing what God will be doing in their lives as they grow up knowing almost first-hand what a different life people live in other countries. Look out world, they are coming soon!

## PREPARING TO LEAVE THE HOME FRONT

It was hard to leave, especially this time, with Brooklyn having some relationship problems with friends. Though we have had our struggles on previous trips and in life at home, Brooklyn and I have grown very close lately. She realizes how some friendships can come and go but certain people you are able to count on. Not fun lessons to learn, but nonetheless, it is good she knows them.

Also making it difficult to leave was the fact that I was out of town from the Wednesday before through the previous Sunday on a trip with Brooklyn to San Diego for her high school choir. It was great fun and great weather, but back-to-back travel is not so fun, especially when you are traveling such great distances!

Also, I hoped that this trip would be a new beginning in Kenya. The last trip left me emotionally devastated, feeling betrayed, and very confused. It was time to try to patch over those previous relationships and to see what God had in store for any potential new relationships.

Looking back, it was a big leap of faith. At the time, I was more focused on getting Laura ready to go and Brooklyn ready for me to leave. I didn't focus too much on it, but there was a lot riding on this trip. It could have led to never going to Kenya again, or it could open doors to new possibilities. Come along and let's see what happens!

*Chapter 5*

# Ending or New Beginnings?
## April 2013: Sue and Laura

If the beginning of a trip is foreshadowing, I'm not sure what to think about this one! It was certainly the most "exciting" adventure traveling to the airport ever. We left early to allow time to grab a last bite of American fast food at a normal dollar amount outside the airport. Mission accomplished! We hit very bad traffic near the airport. There were a lot of weather issues in Chicago that week. Because of the large amounts of rain, streets were flooded, and businesses were closing.

It was raining, hailing, and snowing on April 19th. Our luggage was exposed to the elements in the back of Chris' truck, getting wet the entire ride! We took the final turn off the main freeway that led us to Chicago O'Hare International Airport, which usually takes 10 minutes until we park in the international lot to get our bags out. It was around 7:00 pm when we pulled off the freeway. We were waiting in line for at least an hour with cops coming through the crazy traffic, and we were still not moving at all. At this point, we didn't know if we were even going to make it to the airport on time - 10 minutes away.

Just to give you an idea of how bad it actually was, we witnessed a man start walking down the freeway on the inside emergency lane with his suitcase rolling behind him! If we hadn't had eleven suitcases, we may have done that as well.

By the time we finally got to the international terminal parking area, it was after 8:00 pm. Thankfully, we made it in plenty of time for the flight. We had no problems with any overweight luggage—Turkish Airlines was very generous. We paid for two extra bags, $410, and were off through security, but not before thanking Chris and Darrell for the eventful ride!

## ADOPTIONS

I knew it would be a somewhat stressful trip because there were some much needed meetings at the US Embassy to attend. These meetings were difficult to get, and were to try to help a friend with a situation. Even if I managed to get the meetings, I wasn't sure they would be able to address the issues for my friend. On top of that, there wasn't much time in Nairobi to deal with those issues.

The heartbreaking back-story is this. There was a girl in Kenya, about five or six years old, that was in a difficult and dangerous family situation. Her mom had passed away, her dad had a drinking problem, and there was sexual abuse going on with a neighbor.

Once this was brought to attention through a medical mission, there were alternative arrangements made for her care and safety in Kenya. Generous staff at one of the schools took her in and cared for her. There were a few people from the US that wanted to get the child into the best home situation possible. Hearts were open to bringing the child to the US to take care of her and protect her.

With that as a back-drop, the meetings and/or even the ability to get the meetings, were a very important part of the trip for me. Helping little ones in these situations is near and dear to my heart, and so very important to me. I wanted to be as prepared as I possibly could be to try to get to the correct person to address the questions. I called lawyers in the US who work in the area of international adoption for advice. I researched and researched on how best to approach the office and the problems. I spent hours and hours at home praying, and doing the work. This was my number one priority, and I wasn't sure I was going to be able to pull it off.

I also wasn't sure I had the knowledge to pull it off. I was scared for this little girl, and if I failed, her life would be hanging in the balance. I didn't want to let this poor girl down, or the people back in America willing to do the work of raising her, if that is what is best for her.

Looking back at this situation, I realize that I was trying to play the role of savior for this child. Really all I can do is walk through the doors God opens, and prepare ahead of time for those doors to open. This is what I did and that is all God called me to do. My heart wishes I could do more, but God will take care of the rest.

At my speaking presentations, I get asked all the time about specifics of adoption in Kenya. In Kenya, adoption is a rare thing. It is not overly accepted. People see it as buying/selling babies instead of the legal process that it is. Adoption laws in Kenya are only a little over 10 years old, which in law, is like infancy.

Our partner orphanage, Baby Life Rescue—Peter and Selpher Mutua, specializes in adoption of all their rescue babies. Babies that come to them at a few weeks or months old are usually adopted out before they turn one year. Even some of their older babies are adopted out into great Kenyan families. Adoption is such a rare thing in Kenya, and I am so grateful that God placed Peter and Selpher in our path so we can see the amazing works they are doing for the children of Kenya within the country's own borders.

In Kenya, International adoption is very difficult, but not impossible. After filling out loads of paperwork, which takes hours (true of any international adoption), you can only hope for a timely placement. Once you accept a possible placement child, you have to spend three months in-country bonding. These children are usually only one to two years of age. For international adoptions, the children are on the older end of this age range. After the bonding period, you can go back home, but as the rules stand right now, the child must stay in Kenya. It is understandably difficult for everyone to have just spent three months bonding, and then the child is left for another three to six months without you as you fly home. So the overall process, at the short end, can take a seven to nine month stay in the country, or more regularly, an 18 month stay is required. None of this is a guarantee, and some adoptions take even longer.

I'm hoping God will open doors to talk to the right people about these issues so international adoption can be an option for all the orphans in Kenya. For some perspective on the problem, UNICEF reports approximately 2 million orphans in Kenya alone. Placement with good Kenyan families is great, and we need to continue and further that work. There are many more than can be accommodated this way. However, international adoption would help these orphans find forever families and ease some of the economic hardship that supporting so many orphans places on the country.

There are orphans all over the world. Some statistics say there are more than 13 million of them. I hate that families and children are hurt by the ever changing international adoption policies. I hate even more that children are stuck in unhealthy places that lack the proper funds for food and other necessities, to provide the right kind of care when they are already missing out on all the love that God has for them by not being home with a family.

Say a prayer for them today. Pray that they are safe, well-cared for, and loved. Pray that these childern find a family of their own very soon. Pray that governments will stop changing adoption laws and regulations, and that the US will stand up to protect these laws and the families trying to adopt through them.

In the Democratic Republic of Congo (DRC), adoption regulations have deadly consequences. There, adoptions that have been fully completed by existing processes are not being honored by the DRC government. Parents and children go to finalize the last few pieces of paper to bring the child or children to the US, but the DRC government is refusing to sign them. All that needs to happen is one signature on an administrative visa type document so the children can come home with their new parents to a loving, financially stable, home.

Orphans wait for years for this signature. In the meantime, the parents have to come back to the US. Remember, these parents have already paid $20,000-$30,000 to adopt internationally. They then have to take multiple trips back to the DRC to see if they can push the government for the signature. They have to send more money to cover food and other orphanage fees to try to keep their children as healthy as possible. Parents do all of this without knowing when, if ever, they will get to bring home their child. This is just the financial side of the tragedy and says nothing about the emotional turmoil of bonding with these children, loving them as their own, and then having to leave them behind in conditions that are less than favorable.

The tragedy does not end there. Desperate conditions exist in this country -- civil war, unimaginable poverty, and many other problems -- so there is not enough money for the government to care for these orphans. Some children that are legally adopted by US parents are dying in orphanages due to malnutrition as they simply wait for a government signature on a visa form.

How can this be happening? These orphans are legally adopted pursuant to DRC's own adoption laws. There are a few great organizations working on this international adoption issue, and many other issues.

An organization called Burning Both Ends is attempting to get the US to be more firm on governments trying to change adoption laws mid-way through an adoption process. There is an amazing documentary they have put together called "Stuck". It is available to order on Netflix and online. Mariska Hargitay from Law and Order: SVU narrates the film. They are also doing a lot of work on the DRC adoption issues. I pray God is using their work to change lives of families here trying to adopt, as well as the children left without a family.

Another great organization dealing with orphan issues is the Christian Alliance for Orphans (CAFO). They host an annual conference the first weekend of May which takes place in various cities around the country. The conference brings together people to talk about and address problems for foster care, and also focuses on orphans domestically and internationally. The positive energy that comes through at these events is extraordinary. If these are issues near and dear to your heart, you should commit to going to one of these conferences. Please commit to praying for, and maybe financially supporting, CAFO in their works around the world.

## NAIROBI TIME

No rest for the weary! We arrived in Nairobi at 2:15 am, all luggage accounted for. Yeah! By the time we got to the apartment and finally made it to bed, it was well after 5:00 am. We needed to leave by 10:00 am, so we didn't get much sleep, and were up by 9:15 am. Our first stop was the baby elephant orphanage, operated by the David Sheldrick Wildlife Trust. Here's a small sampling of what their website has to say about their work:

"Born from one family's passion for Kenya and its wilderness, the David Sheldrick Wildlife Trust is today the most successful orphan-elephant rescue and rehabilitation program in the world and one of the pioneering conservation organizations for wildlife and habitat protection in East Africa".

The Wildlife Trust gave us an hour long presentation explaining what they do. The program sends staff out into the wild looking for baby elephants that have been orphaned. As you may know, there is a huge problem with poaching of elephants for ivory tusks leaving the babies without parents. Baby elephants are of no interest to the poachers because they have not yet developed tusks. The baby elephants are fed by large baby bottles that some elephants can even hold for themselves, which is very cute.

Soon after, we were off to an orphanage where there are children that are infants through 18 years of age, located just southwest of Nairobi, in Ngong. The hills in this part of Kenya are gorgeous. Zipporah, the woman who runs this facility, is so sweet and has an amazing story of asking God to provide every day. She started her mission work with her husband, reaching out to kids in a nearby slum area. She then started taking a few kids into their home. It first turned into a co-ed orphanage, then to a primary school, to a farm with crops that the children tended, to a secondary school, and now a church. Today there are 210 kids in the school and 118 in the orphanage.

While at the orphange, we also met Roberta. She was originally born in Illinois but relocated to Arizona years ago. Roberta went on a mission trip with her church in the summer of 2011, and it was during that trip she realized God was calling her to make a difference in the lives of other people. Four months later, on November 3rd, 2011, she sold everything she owned and moved to Kenya permanently. Roberta was in the process of opening a medical clinic on the site of Zipporah's orphanage. She had no specific plans and no commitments for support, just a word from God and the courage to follow, even when it didn't seem to make sense. When we met her, she knew those kids by name and had special connections with them. Not to mention the support she gave Zipporah by being there.

What an inspiration! Are we willing to step out even when it doesn't seem to make sense? Even in little things in life? Take a different route to work, reach out to that friend you haven't heard from in years. Or are we stuck in a rut of doing the same things over and over again? Try something new today!

Day two in Nairobi started with no sleep again, but nonetheless, we were off to New Life Trust baby orphanage that does a lot of adoptions.

Our Mombasa friends, Peter and Selpher, of Baby Life Rescue, ran the Mombasa branch of New Life Trust. New Life wanted to close down the Mombasa branch and move it an hour or two north, but Peter felt that God was calling them to stay in Mombasa, so they turned down the offer. New Life provides very good care for the babies, with lots of interaction, and a schedule for the kids. We fed the 4-8 month olds and got a quick tour before we were off once again.

We had the opportunity to meet with Ms. OJ (Grace) and Ginny. They run a Pregnancy Crisis Center in Nairobi. We learned so much from them about how to lay this type of work out and where to network with others to provide services. They had training and curriculum for working on prevention in the school, which was already approved for use. We just needed to train people on the coast to use it. It was very invigorating to have the chance to see how best to pull everything together in a way that has already shown effectiveness.

They clearly laid out the areas we would need to work in prevention, counseling, and aftervention (work skills training). Having a clear outline of the work helped us think about people to find who could fill various roles. It was great to get feedback on things that had worked, and things that hadn't, so we didn't have to reinvent the wheel and make the same mistakes. We will make our own mistakes, I'm sure, but we can learn from other people's too!

## KIBERA - BENTA

Kibera was next on our agenda, with a chance to see Benta, and the wonderful kids at her preschool. Traffic was maddening in Nairobi.

Kibera is the second largest slum in the world. Benta runs a preschool for HIV positive children and also helps to provide pregnant women with anti-viral medication so their babies have a better chance of being born HIV negative. I like to purchase jewelry and other items from her to help their mission, then I bring it home to sell to raise money for our mission at the Mombasa Pregnancy Crisis Center.

When we arrived, the children were singing for us. The preschool was only a room the size of a large walk-in closet by US standards, maybe 9'x9' or so. There were a few hand-drawn posters on the walls, and only a few books and pieces of chalk. They sang a lot, learned a few songs, and introduced themselves. With Sue, Laura and I all running day care centers, and Laura loving to sing, it was a great fit and a great time for all!

A few of the kids at the school are orphans. For those kids who have no where to go home to, Benta takes them into her own home with all of her own children. Benta herself has HIV, and a few of her children have turned from being HIV positive at birth to being HIV negative.

Benta and her kids are always a joy and bring smiles to our faces. We were able to leave them with some flashcards, crayons, and other supplies for the school.

Sue, Laura, Paul and Rose walked around the streets of Kibera for a while after that. Jayne, the driver, and I went to a meeting with Sylvester, a person who works in Lutheran Missionary work. This was the project that we came to with the vision of building a primary school last summer. Within one hour of discussing the project, the idea of a secondary school came up twice. Now, less than one year later, Ken is at the point of getting a proposal through to the Lutheran Missions Board to help with funding. This meeting was to help bring Ken and his church to the next level.

Soon, we were back at the apartment to gather our bags and head to the airport. It had been raining constantly in Nairobi the week before we came, but while we were there, it did not rain at all. However, as we were driving to the airport, it started to rain again. Great timing.

Our flight to Mombasa was on time, and while in the airport, I sold two books! I almost felt like a real author! One sale was to Mike, who travels placing Bibles in schools, hospitals, and other clinics for Gideon. The other book I sold was to Mercy, who is a member of the Christian Lawyers Association. It was very cool to talk about what we are all doing and to network with them.

We were very excited to get to Mombasa and finally sleep in some comfy beds!

## MOMBASA—HOME AWAY FROM HOME

Our first day in Mombasa always has a lot of running around to do. We have to get food for the house, money exchanged, supplies for our activities, and get all bags repacked for the different centers we will be going to. That, plus jet lag and lack of sleep for two days, led to a difficult time getting out of the house!

Thank God for our driver, Rashid, who helped us with everything. Lucy, Rashid's wife, runs a business cooking meals and selling them to various workers around the area. We thought it would be nice to support her and save money by not eating out as much, so she made us several delicious meals that we threw into the fridge and ate all week as we were hungry.

First on our agenda was to get out to the Valorie McMillan high school near Ingilii School, which was one of Laura's first school visits. We walked through the village around Injilii and went in a few homes.

Note to self—all schools are closed in April in Kenya, so we didn't get to see any classes in session, but we did get to see the schools themselves. School being out was good when visiting the orphanages because all the kids were home all day, but not so good to do activities with the school! I was glad we didn't have any activities planned with the schools.

## GOVERNMENT OFFICIALS INTERESTED IN OUR WORK?

We had an amazing opportunity for a meeting with some important people in Mombasa. Thanks to Pastor Allan, the deputy governor of the area was interested in our project, and I hoped they might help with the funding of our mission. Please pray with us over this and future connections.

Hazel Catana, the Deputy Governor of Mombasa County, thought this was a very unique idea and was anxious to hear more about it. We don't have all the details yet on how our connection will proceed, but she would be coming to our Kenyan run/walk, scheduled for later in this trip. She would be at the starting line to cut the ribbon. As if I wasn't nervous enough about the run/walk, now we had high ranking government official attending who might hold keys to a well-funded organization.

## RUN/WALK IN KENYA - I CANNOT BELIEVE IT

It was an amazing pipe-dream for the run/walk to take place in my hometown of Milwaukee. I cannot believe we were ever able to make that happen, especially considering that we did not have a church base to pull from. In advertising, it was strictly word of mouth and Facebook.

I could not believe we would be hosting a run/walk in Kenya. We went to church at Crossroads, where they were advertising the run/walk on stage during the announcements, and had a meeting regarding the event with Liz, Benna, Mercy, Joy, Jayne and the Kenyan committee. The meeting felt a bit chaotic, which was stressful for me, but we came through alright. It is what it is. Whatever God brings together God brings together. Whatever is left undone is undone.

The night before the event, we had four cakes to bake, 100 certificates to make and sign, a few speeches to write, and we needed to find a ribbon for the Deputy Governor of Mombasa to cut to officially start the race. We were already tired before we started. Working on the ribbon, we hit a few stores and could not find anything. Then we didn't get to Liz's to bake the cakes until after 7:00 p.m. Once we got there, she had the certificates made and ready for Jim to sign. The cakes took half as long to bake than we thought they would, and though we were a little worried on how they would turn out, they turned out perfectly.

Saturday, April 27, 2013, was the day of the run/walk. If I was nervous in the US, you can imagine how nervous I was here not having any control over the situation, except for motivation. I was nervous already, and Rashid, our ever faithful driver, had a punctured tire, so he was late. Being late for anything makes me anxious. When we arrived, all of the tables were already in their correct positions, so we each took a table and started setting up. It went off without a hitch.

The Deputy Governor of Mombasa, Hazel Catana, was present and cut the ribbon at the starting line. She was pulled away on other official business (the president of Somalia came into town that morning), but she arrived to at least do the ribbon cutting and wish us well. You could tell she obviously did not want to leave. We were so lucky to have her. She actually kept the president of Somalia waiting at the airport just so she could be with us!

We had about 40-50 runners, as well as some cyclists. Even more people gave donations to the Pregnancy Crisis Center who were unable to come to the event. Thanks to Liz, Joy, Mercy, Benta, and Jayne for helping to get it going.

We had food and fun. The Crossroads kids did a great skit on the need for a Pregnancy Crisis Center and we had a great time. The Wanna Wa Mola Boys did a great song for us. We had an awards ceremony at the end, cleaned up, debriefed for next year, and headed off to our second baby orphanage.

## WHAT DOES GOD HAVE IN STORE NEXT?

I am so amazed at how God works things out. Unfortunately, the woman who was going to be donating us the land for such a cheap price in Mtwapa, had to put her land up for sale because she couldn't wait any longer. That option was gone. We had already lost long-term relationships with the attorney, Vicky, and psychologist, Hellen, and we were not even sure why. I did have a brief sit-down meeting with Vicky to patch things over—though it was without any explanation of what the problem had been—and to discuss some options for my American friends who might be interested in international adoption.

I was still completely in the dark on what God's next move was for me in Kenya, if there was even going to be any. I knew He wanted me to focus on the Pregnancy Crisis Center, but I did not have anyone well established in that area to coordinate with.

With all the talk at Crossroads Church for the run/walk, two members there indicated I needed to talk to Jane Jilani. Ms. Jilani has had a dream to open a Pregnancy Crisis Center home of this type since prior to 2004. She took the *Equipped to Serve* training that we heard about in Nairobi in South Africa in 2004, and did a one-week internship at two different centers there. She had been working on constructing a building for that purpose, "slowly by slowly", meaning "little by little".

After the run/walk, we got a chance to sit down with Ms. Jilani at the construction site. She put her all into this project, with very little—if any—outside support. She cashed in her retirement account to build the structure that is standing there now. This is saying a lot, because she is retired and supposed to be living off her retirement income. She prays everyday for the funds to feed herself and anyone else who might need it. She is an amazing woman, and very involved in various areas of church work, in addition to her other non-profit works.

I can't believe how God just threw us together! Through the advertising at Crossroads Fellowship of the Pregnancy Crisis Center work, He pulled us together. Five minutes before that, we had no support basis for the work that I knew God was calling for. Then, through no "effort or work" on my part whatsoever, He provided a Kenyan to partner with who shared the same exact vision for the center. There has not been anything that we've disagreed on yet. We have listened to each other, gone over the reasons behind our wants for certain things for the project and have come to an agreement on everything. I am not naive enough to say this will continue forever, but I know we will both turn to prayer if and when we don't agree on something, and will wait for God to work it out. Vicky and Hellen pulled out of the relationship, but God brought someone into my life just as fast to help fulfill His mission in Kenya.

Keep reading as we continue to see how God is working through us on this trip to Kenya!

*Chapter 6*

# The Journey Continues…

## BEING FLEXIBLE

Flexibility is not my strong suit. I am a planner and in the past, I had a tendency to meltdown if the plan was not being followed or if it was suddenly changed. God has used Kenya to pull all that out of me, when I let Him. If left to my own devices, I will plan everything! Kenya is a place where you plan and hope for the best, but you know that things will not work out as planned, so you come in expecting that and learn to "go with the flow".

One morning, we tried to head over to Peter and Selpher's baby orphanage in the morning, but traffic was too jammed, so we ended up heading out to Mtwapa instead. Mtwapa is where George and Mercy run Good Life Center. The amazing orphanage operates like a foster home. It was so great to see them again. I spent a lot of time with George on the last trip and he introduced me to a lot of people. We got another full tour, and it was great to see the kids were growing so well. Everything looked great, and though it wasn't our intended plan for the morning, it was God's plan.

When we were finished in Mtwapa, we came back through town and picked up Rose (from the US, married to Paul), Joy, and Mercy and headed toward Peter and Selpher's place. They just had two little baby girls and a two-year-old girl placed with them.

The two-year-old girl's story is a near tragedy. Her name is Rose. She arrived at Peter and Selpher's orphanage after a prayer group was returning home at 3:00am after a night of prayer, and noticed some dogs barking. This was in December of 2012. After checking out why the dogs were barking the group noticed there was a baby girl laying in the bushes. A mom, desperate I am sure, left her there, unable to care for both herself and her baby.

Rose was brought to Peter and Selpher at Baby Life Rescue to be cared for. They didn't know how old she really was, but based on her molars, the number of teeth, and her height, she had to be around two years old. She was very quiet when we first came, but was laughing and cuddling by the time we left. I would love to take her home with me.

Also with Peter and Selpher was a four-month-old baby girl, Delight Flower. She was found after being abandoned in a flower bed, hence her name. She was only days old when she arrived, and thankfully, was heading out for adoption within the next week.

All of the kids who were there the last time we visited were adopted out already, except one. The only child left was Gift. Gift is a three or four-year-old boy, and has some special needs. He was not yet talking and had an awkward gait. I'm not sure of the specific problems, but they would soon be enrolling him in school and hoping for the best.

On another day, we tried reconnecting with Tammi, Patrick and their baby orphanage. We had been texting back and forth for a day but showed up at their place and were told by the guard that they'd moved. After a few conversations, we realized that they'd moved down by Peter and Selpher (way down, in lots of traffic) where we had been yesterday! This one we had to reschedule, so instead, we headed to Wanna Wa Mola.

Wanna Wa Mola is a boy's home. It is a place where they find boys who are begging or stealing for money to survive on the street, and bring them back to a house, feed, educate, and teach them about God. All the boys love music. They had a few boys come in just the day before. We had such a great time making paper plate tambourines with them. We also gave them kazoos and then talked with them about how God loved them and knew each of their names. We gave them each a cross necklace and wrote their names on them. The boys were patient and very well behaved. It was such a good time. Again, not our plan, but it was God's plan.

Back to the topic of flexibility. We were ready to leave and the car wouldn't start. That's the second time that had happened that same day. We dropped the big van off for repair and had to borrow a friend's car while it was in the shop. Paul came on his motorcycle and helped us. In the meantime, we got a chance to see the boys just play, and be normal boys. Some were doing gymnastics for us.

That was when we noticed Mark. We found out he had just arrived the day before and would not smile. He seemed to want to jump in, but was afraid. We reached out to him a few times, but he kept his distance. Finally, after a several tries, we were able to leave him with a book. He was working hard on learning to read. We had Shadrack read the book to him. Shadrack is a boy who'd been there last time and is going throughout his school sharing the Gospel and having Bible study with the kids. It was cool to see Mark lighten up just a little bit before we left.

It would not have been possible to connect with Mark, a person who really needed a connection at that time in his life, if we stuck to our original schedule. All of these "mishaps" show us that God has His own plan, and if we follow it, amazing things happen. However, if we force our plans, we end up frustrated and angry. The same can be said of our work in the US as well. Flexibility is key. Planning is good, but flexibility is the key.

## EXPANDING OUR FAITH, OR SO WE THOUGHT

The owners of the Neptune, the hotel we stay in when we come with Fox River, support an orphanage for boys. It is very similar to Wanna Wa Mola. Wanna Wa Mola has a huge Christian influence in the work being done there, which we knew before we arrived. We did not think the Neptune would have any Christian influence, as I do not believe the owners are Christian. The plan was to visit with the boys there, similar to our visit at Wanna Wa Mola, which involved reading a very Christian book that a friend wrote, overviewing the entire story of the Bible in a handful of pages.

I would be lying if I said I wasn't nervous. The staff at Neptune was very excited for us to come and did not ask any details about our visit. I would say that all three of us were very nervous about how it would go.

The boys at this home had been there for a very long time, some since 1997. The Neptune actually helps them all the way through to University, or as far as donations allow. We were all a bit nervous as we started our presentation to read our very Christian story of *King Cherish* together. It was the story of Adam and Eve in the garden, all the way through Jesus coming to save us, in just 13 pages. Each boy read a page aloud, and then we talked about what it meant.

We were expecting challenging questions, as we thought they were of different faith backgrounds than what the book portrayed, but God surprised us. We were amazed to see that all the boys labeled themselves as Christian, and the manager did as well. We had such a great time encouraging them and talking with them. At the end, the boys spread out into their own little areas and they wrote out their stories for us to take back home. Some of them even drew pictures for us.

They so enjoyed that time of writing. They asked us a few questions and we left them with more paper and a set of markers to continue to write and draw. They did not want to stop! The boys asked us for Bibles, so we began arranging to get everyone Bibles from the Gideon guy, Mike, whom we had met at the airport. We left the boys with visor hats, cards talking about God loving them, and a few other things as well.

## BARANI—NEW SCHOOL TO ME

We were headed to Barani, a school I had never been to before. It consists of only a very small church and preschool, past Mtwapa, on the way towards Bomani and Vipingo. School had been out of session since after Easter, and the students would not return until May, but it was good to see the size of the place. The school was on only 1/4 of an acre, which was the size of the plot that we tried to get in Mtwapa for the Pregnancy Crisis Center. I was glad we had to change our plans, as that was not very much land at all. We got a chance to see some adorable village children from the area and handed out rubber-band bracelets. They loved just seeing other people. The photo of two of the girls on the cover were taken here.

At Vipingo, Pastor Paul brought all the kids in to sing songs to welcome us. It was nice for Laura to be able to see one school somewhat in session. We taught them a few songs and they taught us a few songs. We all had a great time sitting out under the huge mango tree, which is on the cover of the first book, and enjoying the cool weather. The children were well behaved even without their teachers present. It was so good to see them all and serve them lunch. You could tell they hadn't eaten much in a few weeks because everyone cleaned their plates! Even the little ones ate their whole plate full of food and didn't leave any crumbs behind on the table.

## KIDS PURE LOVE

It is a sad reality for the students that when school is out, a lot of these children get nothing to eat. It is a regular occurrence that kids pass-out, or even faint, during the day on Mondays from lack of food over the weekend. When we visited Vipingo during the school break, I noticed one little girl, whose mom is a teacher at the school, sharing her plate of food with the little girl sitting next to her. Both girls had very full plates of food, but the teacher's child did not go hungry during the weekends because they could afford to buy food. The teacher's little girl knew that the other girl next to her was fed only in school, so she was willing to share her plate of food with her, even though the other little girl already had a full plate of her own. That is just one example of the pure love that flows out of the Kenyan people all the time.

I remember the story of one of our first volleyball games that we had at the centers. It had been raining, so the sand was very muddy, and people were playing in their bare-feet. After the game, one of the players from our team went to the well to wash off her feet before putting her shoes on. One of the little girls from the school ran over to the well and begged her to let her wash her feet for her. Such an amazing example, right from the Bible, of Christ being willing to do anything to show love to someone! He was willing to wash the disciple's feet, even Judas, the disciple that was just hours away from sending Jesus to His death.

We need to remember this story. We need to focus more on serving others and less on our own needs. Serving others leads to a much happier life.

## WHAT A DIFFERENCE A YEAR MAKES - BOMANI WOMEN

In Chapter 4, we left off with the funds which we were able to send to Kenya for the ladies in Bomani to start a small jewelry making business, as well as a Bible study. Thanks to some generous donations, we were able to purchase them the necessary items to start the training to make jewelry. They each had to pay 250 schillings to be part of the group. The ladies would make jewelry, then attempt to sell it. There would be items for sale when Fox River visits, but we also wanted them working on selling items locally so they would have income year round. Liz, a Kenyan who we work with here, might have an outlet for the ladies as well. We got to watch these women in action. They looked great and so happy. They were not making any money yet but being in a community together and in God's Word changed them from the inside out.

This trip we brought some activities to do with the women's Bible studies. They were so excited! Last year, when they were so desperate, and after some of the questions we got, we left thinking they needed to know that they were princesses, that they were Daughters of the King. Sue and I did the *Believing God* Bible study, by Beth Moore, and that lead us to the verse, Isaiah 61:3, where it says:

> "God sent Isaiah to "bestow on them a CROWN of BEAUTY instead of ashes, the OIL of GLADNESS instead of mourning, and a GAR-MENT of PRAISE instead of a spirit of despair".

We had the ladies color crowns that we got free from various Burger Kings around Milwaukee. We had a few jewels and markers and they decorated their own crowns. Then Emily, the Bible study leader, anointed their heads with oil.

Thanks to Joanne Chappel and her business in New Berlin, Chappel Sports, we were able to get a really good deal on t-shirts to send over for each woman. Thank you to all who purchased a t-shirt to help us get them there.

We later handed out little flip mirrors that we got in church when we did the mirror-mirror series. Thank you to Guy and Denise Conn for purchasing those, as there were not a lot left after that sermon series. The ladies were very excited while Emily, the Bible study leader, anointed crosses on their foreheads, and we put the decorated Burger King Crowns on their heads, as well as a pink T-shirt that labeled them each "A Daughter of the King".

We could feel the community spirit between them. They were speaking more English than last time. You could feel a spiritual base coming from them. They were joyful. Even though they still had a lot of prayers for physical needs, you could sense that God was with them and they were no longer desperate.

It was like a night-and-day difference in these ladies. They were like a whole new group when it came time for our question and answer session. The jewelry business would be self-supporting, and it would take a little time to get up and running to produce a profit for them, so none of the changes had anything to do with any immediate economic improvement.

## SOUTH COAST, FINALLY!

My favorite part—South Coast! We headed to Tiwi. I was expecting Fred to have brought some of the kids in to see us as agreed in our previous emails, but no one was there. Luckily, Pastor Vincent met us and took us to his new very small school in the New Mab River area. He's operating on God's grace every day. This was where the newest Operation Give Hope (OGH) well is located, thanks to some generous donors from Fox River - Ron and Wendy Baake.

We also went to see another small school started by Thomas, a man from Minnesota, who moved to Kenya four years ago. Thanks to Thomas, we also got to see a Pregnancy Crisis Center already in motion. It was an amazing place where Kennedy worked. He was awesome and helped us with budget and other information This was the first place we visited that was actually running a live-in maternity home, so they had a better idea of how things worked from a budgetary, financial, and legal standpoint.

## VERY HARD VISIT FOR ME

The day was exhausting, but when we looked back, it didn't seem like we had done a whole lot. We started off by going into the public hospital in Mombasa, Coast General. I hate hospitals even at home, so this was way outside my comfort zone. Judy, who works with an organization called PACK (I'm not sure of the actual words associated with their name) was kind enough to get us into both the Children's Ward, and the Children's Cancer ward. PACK is an organization that goes into the community to find children that need certain cancer treatment, brings them to the hospital and pays for all the necessary medications. The parents only need to pay for the hospital bed. PACK then works to try to reduce the rate for the bed.

There was one little boy in the hospital who had a tumor in his right cheek so big that his eye was turned inward and you could only see white. Judy said that his right cheek was 10 times the size of the other when he started treatment. It was reduced to maybe four times the size of the other cheek by the time we got there.

There was only one option for treating cases like this. Seven steps were outlined on a checklist on the wall in the ward. Those same steps were followed and repeated for all patients. If those didn't work, there were no other options. Every person gets the same treatment regiment, no matter what. It was very much a checklist situation, and if you didn't fit into the checklist, you were asked to leave. Very sad.

Like all other buildings in Kenya, the hospital was an open air facility. The ward beds were very dirty. There were flies everywhere, and you could see dust drifting in from construction work being done within the hospital. With all the construction and street traffic, it was also very noisy. The ward was full of children, most with their mothers, but a few of them had their dads sitting with them.

Not much was going on to help anyone while we were there. We saw one doctor talking to one of the mothers for about five minutes. While we were there, the nurses briefed us a little bit, but I did not see them doing anything except standing at the nurse's station, talking, and cleaning the station.

We handed out Burger King crowns to all the kids and some of the parents. That brightened their day a little bit. One boy was so skinny he couldn't even lie down on the bed he was in so much pain. They thought he might have a heart condition, but he looked very malnourished. There were some very tiny babies there as well.

Judy shared with us that the hospital gets very over-crowded sometimes. When this happens, they assign two patients to one bed. Can you imagine? You are so sick that you take yourself to the hospital, but then they are so crowded that they put you in a bed with a complete stranger? Judy indicated that people also have to bring someone to stay with them in the hospital because they are short on nurses. This means the person who comes with you must help you get to the bathroom if needed, or other things like that. Food is also not something the hospital provides for patients.

Imagine this for a moment if you can. Checklists on the wall for your treatment plan, open air facilities with dust and construction going on all around, dirty beds and flies everywhere, two people to a bed, very little attention, having to bring a friend to sit with you the length of your entire stay and help you go to the bathroom, and bring your own food if you have it. This is the reality of life for many people in the world. Again a reminder of how much we have to be grateful for.

The hospital was hard to see, and it took a lot out of me. I have dreaded hospitals ever since I was once hospitalized for eight days with a blood clot in my leg and in my lungs. In a hospital, I feel like I am in a prison and unable to get out. Add to that seeing childhood cancer and all of the other conditions, it totally wiped me out. I know I could never be a nurse of any kind, so I am grateful to those who are. I'm also grateful to people like Judy, who while not a nurse, is treated by the hospital staff as though she were a doctor and had all the answers for cases they didn't have answers for.

## UPDATE ON ADOPTION MEETINGS FOR LITTLE GIRL

Remember Mercy, one of the two people that bought my book in the Nairobi airport? We had a chance to visit her and talk about international adoption issues. Mercy is a law school professor and she practices family law! That is the area of law I practiced as a lawyer. She is very knowledgeable in talking through guardianship vs. child custody vs. international adoption and what would work best in the specific situation we were looking into. It looked like we may have been able to get this taken care of after only a few weeks in the country, a process that, if done any other way, would take 9-18 months.

The US Embassy is the key to this whole process. We needed the embassy to issue the child a visa with a child custody order, and an adoption order. However, the Embassy phone number we had would not go through. I received a response to an email earlier that morning that was not helpful at all. I would have to deal with that by email when I got home. This was not the success I'd been hoping for. I would be back in June, so hopefully we might be able to arrange something then, if not by email prior to that.

## MEETING TO UNVEIL PREGNANCY CRISIS CENTER

It was as if God had placed the same exact vision in both of us, Jane Jilani and I. It just took us several years to meet. She started this work in the early

2000's. I had started working in Kenya in 2010, and wasn't clear on God's vision for me until the summer of 2012.

Jane had already started construction on the center in Bamburi, an area just outside the city of Mombasa, in the same county. The first floor was just about finished, and she anticipated adding two more floors. As I said before, she has poured her entire retirement fund, and more, into this building. She came out of retirement to run a few small businesses to raise the funds to keep things moving in the school, and for her family.

We are praying for the government to allow the transfer of land out of one name into another, and dividing the land as needed for the project to continue. We probably needed around $37,000 to finish the second floor, a similar amount for the third floor, and then some funds for finishing off the first floor with drywall. This was so exciting! I could not believe it!

After the Kenyan run/walk, we wanted to make the most of the exposure and asked people interested in volunteering with this project to join us at a meeting on the 1st of May, which is Kenyan Labor Day (public holiday). It was a good turn-out, for a public holiday, with very engaging discussions on how to approach prevention issues and other topics.

We had some very key people who came and were looking forward to getting the training started. George, the social worker for Good Life Orphanage, came to volunteer and help us get organized from the social-work aspect. I am grateful for him. He is an amazing social worker and is especially good at organizing, starting organizations, and getting books and files together.

After the meeting, I was able to speak with Barbara Porter, an American who has been planting Pregnancy Crisis Centers all over Africa, and has been in Kenya for a while. She is amazing! Barbara is giving us an amazing deal to come out and provide training on counseling for the volunteers. I can't believe things are falling into place so easily. She is even paying her own airfare to get here! We just need a place for her to stay.

## STARTING TO SAY GOOD BYE

Earlier in the week, right after the run/walk, we were finally able to stop in and say hello to Patrick and the babies. The same babies were there as the last time we visited. They were growing up, but they looked skinny. They moved from a bigger place in Nyali to a much smaller place in a not so great neighborhood. We are praying for them.

A few days later, we headed back, and it was time to say goodbye. We enjoyed seeing Selpher once again. Selpher came with us over to Patrick's orphanage so we could introduce them. I look forward to them working together on getting the children into permanent long-term homes through adoption, and just giving spiritual and emotional support to each other.

I went again to meet with Jane Jilani and Jayne Claire, to discuss further details on the future of the property and Pregnancy Crisis Center. We had a great meeting, got a lot of details worked out, and came up with a long "to do" list to follow up with; training, building details, financial support for the building and the girls, website, Facebook page, and many other things. I'm very excited to see where this takes us.

### MARK - A HEART CHANGED BEFORE OUR EYES

Sue and Laura had a great time at Wana Wa Mola dropping off some extra things and saying good-bye. We'd met Mark last week and saw him again at the run/walk where all the boys came and ran. Remember when we first arrived, he would hardly look at us, and flat out firmly refused to smile.

But now, just a week later, he was really opening up to us. He wanted to know the exact details of when we would be visiting them again. He was smiling and having a great time. It was great to see God working changes in him so quickly.

### JOB

We met with Job at Crossroads. Job used to work in the shopping centers, making soapstone and selling various curios. His boss was not happy when he became a Christian that he could no longer overcharge or lie to customers.

Job ended up having to quit his job and came to work for a lot less pay at Crossroads Church as the gardener. His wife and kids live a long distance away from Mombasa. Job is struggling to get enough money together to visit them, and also struggles with school fees for his children. I will be working with him to make woodwork and soapstone that I can bring back to sell so he has some extra income coming in. I can get a good deal at the same time.

## SUSAN—MOTHER'S VISION

George, from Good Life Orphanage, introduced us to Susan in Mtwapa. She is opening a rescue center there called "Mother's Vision". After meeting with her, we realized what she is doing is more like an orphanage. She is specifically targeting kids that have been raped or sexually abused.

Susan has a building and all the necessary documents/permits, etc. They are only waiting for finances to provide work staff and a little for food. They have 60 children on a waitlist hoping to get into her facility. It is quite a colorful place. Moses, the pastor there, sat with us and we talked and prayed. It was a great end to the day.

Susan needs to write a book about her life story. She was pregnant at 15 and living in the streets, which is her motivation to start this center. Her story is an inspiration.

## NAIORBI PREGNANCY CRISIS CENTER WITHOUT LIVE-IN FACILITIES

We visited Nairobi for one last day in Kenya. First, we said one last goodbye to Benta and a few of her kids and to drop off flashcards and other school supplies so she can continue her work in the nursery school. Then we visited Ginny's Pregnancy Crisis Counseling Center in the outskirts of Nairobi. It was great to see the work they do! They are very willing to help us train our girls on paper bead jewelry and other items.

We tried to see a Pregnancy Crisis Center that houses women for short periods of time, but we were not able to make that work because of heavy traffic.

For dinner, we went to KFC (they call it Kenya Fried Chicken here!) for an early dinner at 3:00 pm and then headed back to the apartment to get some sleep. We had to get up at 1:00 am to be at the airport on time for our 3:45 am flight. Well rested and ready to go, it was off to the airport.

## BIGGEST TAKE AWAY FROM THIS TRIP

I think the biggest take away from this trip is probably GOD'S WAY. On the last trip, everything fell apart, and it looked like our work may not have been able to continue in Kenya. Since then, I've written a book about my travels, and it brought clarity to what God was calling me to do. This whole time, I knew, that in the end, we would be working on a Pregnancy Crisis Center after we got the adoption work started. Looking back, ever since the first blog in October 2010, a pregnant girl in trouble who contacted me after reading a very generic post, and I saw the need. That need has since been confirmed with various professionals (lawyers, doctors, government officials, and others) who have indicated there are no such agencies in Mombasa, and they are greatly needed.

I can see now why God pulled me away from Vicky and Hellen and their wonderful work on adoption. He used the first book to show me the way He wanted me to move. I've done a lot of soul searching. It feels like God's timing is coming together. Jane Jilani has been waiting on this Pregnancy Crisis Center since 2004, when she first took the training, and received the land from the government. It feels like God is bringing everything together.

God's way. I wonder what He has in store for the next trip, which is only a little over a month away?

# FROM LAWYER TO MISSIONARY:
*The Journey Continues*

Scrapbook | Kenya 2012 - 2015

## June 2012: Community Day

*Carrie (above) and Pam (below) with the kids*

Ken                Number of people at Community Day

*Mini construction crew -
distributing hats*

*Good friends*

*Cooking & feeding everyone*

## June 2012: School, Tiwi

*Lesson on God protecting us better than our hats and reading a bible verse on God's protection*

*Tiwi outside activity - jacks*

*Tiwi outside activity - basket ball*

*Tiarras and good friends*

# Schools

*Classroom - little ones at Viping*

*All kids at Tiwi*

*The Tiwi Choir*

*Teachers and Tiwi baseball hats*

*Perani - gifts of balls*

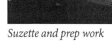

*Suzette and prep work*

*Carrie & Nicole catching up after Bible study*

*Vipingo Bible study*

90

*Presentation - little ones*

*Tiwi graduation - little ones*

*Tiwi graduation certificate with Jim*

*Tiwi graduation ceremony in church*

# Food

Handing out lunch boxes

Pam cooking food

Food and education brings
hope & SMILES!

Food being prepared at schools
in Kenya & a favorite dish.

# Free School

*Most children go without shoes and have limited clothing*

*Pam and Carrie at the free school handing out shoes*

*The children of the free school showing their new shoes*

## Pregnancy Crisis Center

*Girls to help*

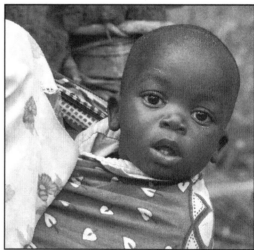

*Jane Jilani building*    *Adorable baby*

## Village Life

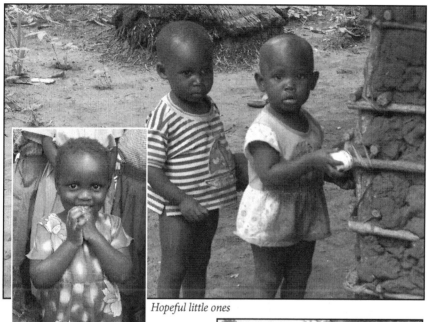

*Hopeful little ones*

*Handing out lunch boxes*

*Carrying wood on her head*

*Little girls carrying babies*

95

## Shoes

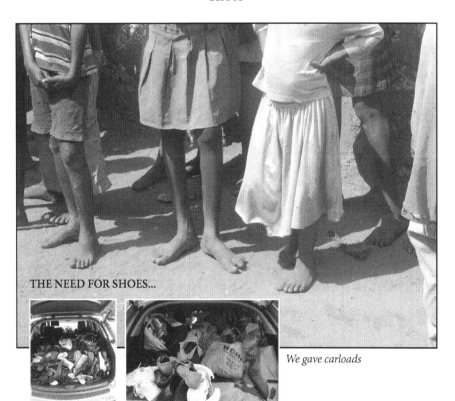

THE NEED FOR SHOES...

*We gave carloads*

*Shoe handout*

*Black garbage bags to gather shoes into*

# Benefit Run 2012

*Starting line & back of the T-shirt*

*Beautiful sunrise*

*Chris setting up the tables*

*& crafts and the Alverno girls*

97

## Benefit Run Kenya 2013

*T-shirt pick up and setting up*

*Hazel Katana, Deputy Governor of Mombasa, coming to cut ribbon*

*Winners!*

*Carrie presenting awards*

# Kenya Culture

*Kenya country of constrasts - housing, childrens' only outfit, a beautiful flower.*

City streets

*Lots of kids getting a lift*

## Village Life

*This girl is Carrie's computer screen saver reminding her of all the girls out there still needing help.*

*Sue Huerta and the family she "adopted" in Bomani, Kenya*

# Village Life

*Those still waiting to get into the school, stealing
a glance through the gate*

*Village girl in Vipingo*

*Sue Huerta reading a book to Faraja Orphanage children*

*Zipporah's orphanage near Nairobi in the Ngogn Hills*

*Chapter 7*

# Shoe Lady!
## June 2013: My Mom

My tenth trip to Kenya was a Fox River trip, June 18-28, 2013. I decided to go on this trip because my mom was coming along. This is not the first trip I've taken with my mom. In March 2011, we traveled together to Israel with Fox River and we really enjoyed it. My mom has done so much to help support all our work in Kenya. She's held rummage sales at her house. She's supported us by sending toys, hats and other things to the children in Kenya. She's even gone so far as to help with the day care at home while I travel and helps take care of my kids! She has also donated food for spaghetti dinners, she has sacrificed much of her time. I'm so glad she will now finally be able to experience the fruits of her labor first-hand by traveling with me to Kenya.

Unfortunately the trip was marked by a lot of long rains and not the typical tropical rain "hard-for-five-minutes-and-then-blow-over" kind of rain we're used to. We persevered nonetheless.

I couldn't help but think of the ironic mix of blessings and distress that rain brings to the people living in the villages. Without the rain, crops do not grow. If crops do not grow, people do not eat. Most people in the villages raise their own food, eat some of it, and sell/barter the rest.

At the same time, the hard, pouring rain, are not always the best for the crops and it also causes irreparable damages to homes. When it rains in America, we usually don't have any worries. For Kenyan villagers, their homes literally wash away. The people cannot afford to rebuild, and most are inside on mud floors getting wet as the rain pours straight through a roof made from dried out palm tree branches. Reliable shelter is yet another thing we have to be grateful for that I rarely acknowledge or think about.

## THE TRIP

We spent time at the Fox River School in Vipingo and the free government school in Bomani. My mom and I taught the baby class at Bomani, which is actually made up of three-year-olds. We made visors, handprint art (an activity I saw on the walls during my next trip), played balloon catch, and blew bubbles. It was a fun day for the kids.

Then another harsh reality struck. Ester, one of the little girls in the baby class, was leaving school early with some relatives. Her mom passed away that morning. While we were playing with Ester, her mom was home in her hut dying of AIDS. Her relatives were there to figure out where she would live and how everything would play out for Ester, because her dad had already passed away. Three years old and no parents. It is just a harsh reality of life in Kenya. Life is not easy. These situations again remind us of how we need to pray for the children and be grateful for our lives.

On this trip, Fox River added something new. We were able to take the sixth graders on a field trip to the Hollar Park Zoo in Mombasa. The children were so excited! Most of them had never been to the zoo, and for some of them, it was their first trip in a van. So we all partnered up and walked around the zoo all day, each of us with three or four students. It was a lot of fun watching the kids and getting to know them. Best of all, the kids really enjoyed it. We even got to feed a giraffe out of our own hands! They have purple tongues that feel like a cat's, and their necks seem so much longer when they're up close and personal.

My mom and I pulled away for a day to go to South Coast and spend some time in Tiwi and at Peter and Selpher's Baby Life Rescue orphanage. We did bubbles, photos for the sponsorship website, and lacing with the kids in Tiwi. It was great to share my favorite places with my mom. We didn't have much time at the baby orphanage, but it was great to say hi.

At the two big community days at Vipingo and Bomani I had a chance to see Mark again from Wanna Wa Mola. He looked so happy. It was awesome to see! The boys were on stage performing some of their music, which was such a treat to watch! However, the rain did put a damper on this event too.

This is where, on later reflection, I had the biggest take away from this trip. A friend of mine, Pam, came to Kenya the year before. Her daughter, who had health struggles most of her life, passed away at a young age. She took a leap of faith with God to come on the trip, which was a difficult one for many reasons. While she was in Kenya, in both Vipingo and Bomani, there were several girls around her daughter's age that really took to her and surrounded her with love. On this current trip, the girls were all coming up to me asking if Pam was there. It seemed they were more anxious and excited than normal for kids who routinely come up and ask if certain people they remembered from before came back or not. They also had their hands filled with gifts for her, various notes and other small things to share with Pam. It showed me how much of an impact Pam made on them.

Though I was not thinking about anything in particular, God showed me how he gave Pam three or four additional daughters similar in age to her daughter, to watch grow up before her eyes a half a world away. It was as if her daughter was up there with God orchestrating this and helping Pam keep moving forward. Pam is an amazing example of how to trust in God, even in difficult times, to find comfort and strength to carry-on. She is a bright shining example of Christ while she does it. I am so grateful to have her in my life.

## ADOPTION / BREAKING HEARTS

Back at the hotel after one of our days in the villages, we met with a lawyer to further discuss the little girl who needed a family home after some struggles with her dad and abuse happening with her neighbor. After a very long, detailed meeting, and a lot of prayer, it was decided that it would be best for the little girl to not come to the US, but to instead stay in safe quarters in Kenya. A move to the US at her age would re-traumatize her with culture shock on top of the trauma she had already experienced by losing her mother, as well as the sexual abuse by a neighbor. The person who opened her heart to the little girl knew that was what God was asking, but her heart was breaking at the same time. She had thought of this girl as her soon-to-be daughter for months. She knew God had other plans for her and the little girl, but her heart was bleeding.

Because of her commitment to the little girl, this person is planning a year-long visit to Kenya. She will spend her year sharing her education background and training with the many schools in Kenya, especially focusing on educating little ones, which will be such a blessing for our schools. Though God did not call her to the adoption she was open to, He led her to something even larger. She was willing to acknowledge that and not push something through which would not have been in the best interest of the little girl or her, even though her heart wanted it. She is a great example of letting go of our wants in order to leave room for what God wants us to do. It will be bigger and better than any of our wants could ever be.

## SEEING THE NEED FOR THE PREGNANCY CRISIS CENTER FIRST HAND

While we were looking at the Fox River farm in a little village near Mombasa, there was a young girl, maybe 15, who had a teeny-tiny baby with her. This young girl was so full of undeserved shame, she could not even look anyone in the face. Jayne Claire was able to get a little of her story once we walked away. Her father had sexually abused her, leaving her pregnant. He left the family when she started "showing". She is shunned by her mom, because her dad left "because of her". In her mother's eyes, there was a little hope when the father was there to help bring in money to the family unit. But now that he was gone, for better or worse, there is even less hope of feeding and taking care of the family. This young girl had been abused horribly by her father and now was raising a baby as a constant reminder of all this. At the same time she was being shunned by her remaining family. She is not in school and has no chance of making a living outside of her mother's home. Here is an example of why the Pregnancy Crisis Center is so needed here in Kenya.

## MOVING FORWARD WITH PREGNANCY CRISIS CENTER

Since leaving in May, Jane Jalani (JJ) and Jayne Claire worked together and with others to keep things moving. JJ's daughter, Mbeyu, has been very instrumental to the project's progress. She's been working really hard in a lot of areas, especially in the rehabilitation area, getting job trainers for the girls at the center. JJ and Mbeyu have a lot of non-profit experience working in this area, so they are very familiar with the who, what, where and when of what needs to happen. We are so grateful to have them.

We dealt with some issues on the land and getting fill for it, worked on getting our hands on a Kenya Youth for Christ - *Worth the Wait* Training manual for our prevention work, and poured over contractor estimates for continued work on the building.

There were differences of opinion on a few issues, but God was able to work it out. We also met with George from Good Life. George is a social worker who is working with us on policies and procedures and in any other way he can. He is going back to school to further his education and is praying for support to pay for his schooling while he volunteers his time to help various non-profits start up. Scott, from the US, offered to help with the website for the project, which was completed in time for our next trip.

## FUNDING, FUNDING, FUNDING -
## THE CONSTANT STRESSOR

Jayne Claire and I met with Bruce O'Neil, who is the founder and director of Manna Worldwide. They are an amazing group. They travel the world looking for great, sustainable, long-term mission projects, and then come to the US to help with funding. They currently fund the food at our schools in Kenya, and they also have lots of other projects in many countries around the world. Orphanages are a large part of what they do.

Through this trip, God also graciously provided us with a sponsor who is helping to support the administrative portion of the work as we try to get things up and running. We are so blessed! Thank you, thank you, thank you! If not for this sponsorship, we would not be as far along as we are.

It is so hard to find people willing to help with the administrative part of the organization. Everyone likes to see the end result and wants every dollar to go to the girls (which is what we want, too), but there is the reality of needing to have cell phone minutes to call a cab to get the girls to the hospital at night, or that we need a copier and other office supplies to continue working. To have someone willing to donate to these necessary administrative portions of the work is very special to us, and means so much. We're also very grateful for all our committed volunteers. We could not do this work without all of you.

## HOME AGAIN

The biggest take away from this trip was the stories of other's struggles turning into triumphs: Pam, with her daughter and her now added Kenyan daughters, the person willing to adopt a girl who had been through a lot in her short five or six-year life, but who also was willing to let her stay behind in Kenya when God called her to do so.

Upon returning home in early July, 2013, it was full steam ahead on fund raising. Between grant writing proposals, run/walk preparations, and a shoe drive, I was very busy. However, the run/walk was my top priority. Writing letters for sponsorship, getting the website and registration stuff ready, marketing to participants, and so much more. Just to assemble the bare basics to get the run officially up and running took one week of full-time work and that does not include ordering T-shirts, other administrative work, and all the extra details.

Thanks again to the amazing Alverno students from the winter semester. Without them, this year's race would not have happened. Aramark also chipped in with food donations. Financial donations for the medals came from Bill's Roofing and Siding Service and Thomas F. Roepsch, CPA. All came through to support the run. Also, thanks to R&K Support Services, Inc. and my Kenya friend, Rosie (Rosie hosts the medical mission trips through Fox River, holding clinics at all the Operation Give Hope schools). These supporters help cover our overhead expenses so the event can take place! Thanks again to my amazing mom, we were able to get this event together, as I was in Kenya when T-shirts needed to be ordered and other items needed to be dealt with.

We also decided to add a silent auction this year. Last year, we did a raffle, and it was nice, but the auction, we thought, might generate more money for the cause. We had amazing response in donations locally, with The Jewelry Store donating a very nice necklace, Liberty Tax Service a certificate for a free tax return, and a really nice quilt from Hales Corners Lutheran's quilting group.

To make it the most effective auction possible, we wanted to do a pre-auction event on Facebook. The items were photographed and uploaded, but we struggled with figuring out what kind of page to make it and how to get enough visibility. Needless to say, this idea was a tremendous waste of time, except for the lessons we learned in the process. We were having a lot of trouble getting it up off the ground. We would love to find help in the area of online silent auctions for future events.

After the event, a friend of a friend, Irene, came over to me and asked if I wanted help doing a bigger and better silent auction. She indicated that she had solicited donations for silent auctions previously for her children's school and would be happy to help. With her help, we decided to do another large fund raising event with a silent auction in the spring of 2014.

The silent action is a simple example of how a "failure" can turn out to be a blessing. The silent auction did not work. We put a lot of time and effort into soliciting donations, picking up donations, taking pictures, uploading pictures, making up rules and descriptions, etc. and it just didn't work out. Instead, God brought us someone to help do it right in the future, and run a separate spring fund raiser for Operation Give Hope.

What looked to be a failure turned out to be a huge blessing. We need to look at all situations in life this way. We might not understand why certain things happen in the moment and it might take some time to see certain situations from another perspective, but there is always another perspective. Stick with it, and you will find the silver lining.

## SHOES

As we talked about earlier, lack of shoes is a major world health crisis according to the World Health Organization. Lack of shoes results in infections, as well as many other problems, like keeping kids out of school because they lack the proper uniform.

Shoes are something most of us have 20-30 pairs of in each of our closets. Some of them we rarely, if ever, use. Shoes are extremely valuable. They change lives in other parts of the world.

We've held a few shoe drives in previous years, collecting money to purchase shoes locally in Kenya which we can then hand out directly to people who need them. When holding these drives, we found people would rather donate shoes, but we just didn't have the ability to ship them or carry them in our luggage.

Fortunately, shortly before we left for Kenya on this trip, I received an email from an organization called Funds2orgs.com. They encourage non-profit organizations to host shoe drives, paying the organization $0.40 for the shoes they collect. Funds2orgs then takes the shoes around the world, focusing right now on Haiti. When I heard about this, I thought, "That sounds like fun. How hard can it be, right?"

So, Jesi Epsie, an outstanding partner for Operation Give Hope for over six months, agreed to work with me on this project. Up until this point, Jesi had been helping us mainly with graphic design work. I can't even begin to tell you how many projects she has completed for us, ranging from flyers to table topper designs, and so much more. All donated. Without her, we would not be at the point we are. Her work is second to none and she does it with such passion and flair.

We met weekly to discuss places we could place big red boxes for shoes, and then made phone calls to start making them. Jesi Epsie's husband, Tim, suggested a place called "Innovative", a gym/workout facility in Franklin, Wisconsin. They were very receptive. Within one week, we had a box inside Innovative and shoes were pouring in. A few weeks later, a good friend, Larry, stopped by and suggested the Southwest YMCA as a host for a box. Once placed, shoes started pouring in even faster. Through Facebook, a friend indicated that her Curves fitness facility would like to host a box. Shoes came in droves! The shoe donation drive had become so successful, I had to have someone empty the boxes two to three times per week while I was in Kenya. Thank you to my volunteers and friends: Sue Huerta, Mara Demien, Suzette Svensen, Cathy Reynolds, Julie Stubenrauch, and so many others who collected and/or picked up shoes for us!

Also through Facebook, I was introduced to a wonderful chiropractor, Jodi Osborne of Osborne Chiropractic, in Hales Corners. She led an amazing effort at her chiropractic office that resulted in the donation of over 630 pairs of shoes! Hales Corners Lutheran Primary School also collected a lot of shoes. The Hales Corners Lutheran Elementary School collected over 500 pairs. Another Catholic school in Hales Corners collected a similar amount.

Martin Luther High School also held a shoe drive, and although their numbers were not the highest, the weight of shoes was off the charts! Lots of "like-new" high school boy-sized basketball shoes. Friends and family brought shoes too. Every night, I would come home to a few bags of shoes on my porch or by my garage. People were holding drives at their workplaces and through their children's sports teams.

Brooklyn and I spent hours each night driving to different locations to pick up the shoes, putting 20-25 per bag. We collected over 600 bags by December, 2013. My garage was so full at one point, you could not see the ceiling. The drive was originally scheduled to run from July through the end of October 2013, so we could have our garage back for the Wisconsin winter. We were hoping to have 300 bags by the end of July, but it was a slow start and we didn't even have 100 bags by that date. They have poured in since and continue to do so. Fortunately, we were able to get Tess Corners Storage to donate a storage facility for the shoes through the end of January 2014, so we have been able to continue.

It was amazing to see everyone pull together to make such a huge difference. The shoes went to Haiti to make a life changing difference by helping people start small businesses and support their families. Through this shoe drive effort, Operation Give Hope has already made nearly $5,000 toward our Pregnancy Crisis Center. We have collected 572 bags of shoes which amounted to an incredible 12,870 pairs!

The drive has been so successful at bringing in funds, and the donations sites have expressed so much interest in hosting the boxes again next year, we think we will be making this a yearly thing. If anyone wants to do a drive in their hometown, let me know—it does not need to be close to Milwaukee. They will come pick up from your location if you can get 100 bags of 20-25 pairs of shoes. It is super simple and easy. The hardest part is making a few phone calls to some gyms, chiropractors, or schools, and putting up a few posts on Facebook. We have all the marketing you need.

It is amazing how fun it is to do a shoe drive. The key is to find a place where people go a few times a week—work, gym, chiropractor, day care, school. This helps them remember to bring the shoes. It was really cool to see people who normally don't donate to international causes open up to this opportunity and get behind it full force! God was really opening a lot of doors.

## WHAT'S NEXT?

Between all of this, I had to get the next trip ready to roll. Colton was coming and we had a last minute addition of another friend of a friend, Suzette. Timing wise, it was difficult, but everything came together. Funds were very tight on this trip as there was not enough time to do any fundraising. It is hard to do certain fund raisers in the summer with crazy schedules but, nonetheless, we had the tickets purchased in mid-July, and were preparing to depart the end of September.

The third trip of the year was only two and a half short months away and it was going to be one of the most difficult trips ever.

## Chapter 8

# Terror Attacks and Rough Edges
## September 2013: Colton and Suzette

Trip number eleven would consist of me, my son, and a friend I met in July, Suzette. This being the third trip in five months time, I felt like I was spending more time in Kenya than in the US! It was a bit difficult because it takes awhile to plan the trip itself. A lot of quiet time and prayer time is needed to make sure I am following God's lead on things, and not my own. In addition to the quick turn-around on the last two trips, I was also in the middle of planning, executing, and marketing for the Second Annual Run Walk for African Orphans which was to take place in Milwaukee on October 18, 2013. We left the US on September 25 and returned home on October 10, just days before the run/walk. Everything for that needed to be ready before I left. Thanks to my mom for all her help.

### SAFETY IS ALWAYS FIRST

We came to Kenya amid great terror attacks and with some fear, and lots of fear from those around us. In Nairobi, on September 21, 2013, less than one week before we got there, horrible terror attacks occurred at a Western style shopping area - Westgate Mall. In the attacks, 67 people were killed and 175 were injured. Al-Shabaab, a Somalia-based Islamic terrorist group, claimed responsibility.

Somalia borders Kenya to the northeast. Besides Al-Shabaab, there is a hate relationship for many Somalian people towards Kenya for various reasons. First are the refugee camps in Northern Kenya. A few years before, due to substantial drought conditions, there was a famine in Northern Kenya. Somalians were also struggling with drought, but at the time Somalia was not recognized as a state by the rest of the world, so they did not get any help. This caused a lot of tension between the two countries.

Another sore spot for Somalia has been the role that Kenya played to help keep pirating problems in check. These are the same pirates that spurred the Captain Phillips movie. Somalia is not happy Kenya is working with the rest of the world, so they take out their frustration in the form of terror attacks, mostly in Nairobi.

In Mombasa there are problems as well. The first day we arrived, which was a Friday, the Muslim holy day, there was rioting in the streets of downtown Mombasa. We were asked to leave the food court of Niava's shopping center because they did not want people to stick around for more than one or two hours at a time. We were having a meeting with our pregnancy crisis team that we ended up having to move to another private location for safety reasons. From then on we held all further meetings at our place of residence for safety.

A semi-high ranking public official was killed early in the morning in the town of Mwtapa. We had just traveled through the evening before the killing occurred. On the second Friday we were there, again the Muslim holy day, more rioting took place in the streets very near our driver's home. We were forced to stay home all afternoon.

In Mombasa, it appears that most of the violence is actually perpetrated by young political activists who attempt to use the religion angle of Muslim vs. Christian to start violence and get people to side with them in their political views. Kenya is a Third World country, and does have safety concerns. A look at the US State Department website confirms this. The situation is not as bad as some countries in Africa in the midst of civil war, or having no semblance of control over anything, but there are safety concerns.

Safety is our foremost concern. This is why we always travel with a Kenyan local national, usually male, and we try to have more Kenyans than Americans in our group at all times. We also avoid malls as much as we can. Avoiding anywhere lots of people gather is an important safety tip. We continually ask Rashid, our driver, for advice on what to do and not do, and always follow his leading and guidance. Of course prayer is always our first line of defense. We also register with the State Department so we get warnings from them about what is going on. Also, if we needed to be evacuated, they will come and find us and usher us out.

The hotels are probably one of the safest places to be. The tourism industry produces the most jobs for the people of Kenya. Kenyans can make a living as cooks, repair men, desk clerks, guards, and other hotel staff. Hotels are a big business for good upstanding business owners.

Even the "bad guys" want to protect the hotels. Sex-trafficking is a huge problem everywhere in the world, but especially in Africa. Mombasa, as a major port city, increases the problem. I pray continually about the horrible things being done to children through sex-trafficking. It is an awful industry that does evil things. And it is an industry - if there wasn't a market for children, this would not be happening. In this case, it does help increase safety in hotels. Neither the good guys or the bad guys want to mess with the hotels because it is bad for business to do so. This makes hotels the safest places in Kenya.

This particular trip, we were not sure if we would go to Nairobi because it was unclear if the Westgate Mall situation was fully resolved. My Kenyan friends in Nairobi had indicated to me that it was resolved, but our news sources in the United States were unclear about it.

Given the random attacks in the Mombasa area, I almost canceled going to church knowing that the political activists in Mombasa have been using religion to spread fear, and because church draws a large crowd of people who might be targeted. However, after hearing how the church starts a safety patrol the night before with people constantly searching the area for items and people, we ended up going to the less busy service anyway. The safety patrol even continues through every service and includes searches of every car.

Despite these situations, I do not come to Kenya with fear. I know God will lead me and guide me if I watch for His guidance and awareness at all times. I am not afraid. Any day could be my final day, but as we have seen in previous chapters in this book and the last - we don't know when our last day will be. My final day could come riding in my car or sitting in my house. Life is short, and we should be living every minute as if it were our last, because it may well be. If we live our lives like this - we trust God to take care of us and know that when it is time, it is time. Fear is a time stealer and unnecessary. Live in the moment, and for the moment, as if it is your last, and you won't regret a thing.

## NAIROBI

After much prayer and reflection, we did decide to take the Nairobi trip after all. We finally got to meet Maureen, a woman who grew up as a child sponsored by Compassion International. She was sponsored all the way through college, earned a degree, and is now running a pregnancy center in Nairobi similar to the one we are looking to start. She has partnered with an American from Texas on this venture. We spent almost the whole day hearing about how they got started and about their programs. Maureen has so many amazing God stories. We also were able to see the girls making paper-bead necklaces, which was very cool and made me even more excited to sell them.

## SOUTH COAST

Because we stayed overnight in a beautiful cottage right on the ocean, we got to do a few more things in South Coast. Special thanks to Jayne Claire for hooking us up with the cottage.

Spending time in Perani and Tumani, two other Operation Give Hope schools on South Coast, was nice. It was only my second ever visit to Perani. Suzette brought soccer balls and bubbles and we also brought a donation of volleyballs from the Southwest YMCA. Normally, people don't get very excited about volleyball or netball in Kenya. But we had a lot of balls for this school and a few of them were volleyballs. It turns out that they LOVE playing volleyball at this school. The teachers and kids play everyday at all recess times. Lacking balls to play with, they had just started resorting to playing with a bunch of plastic bags tied together with a string. That is something the kids do for soccer balls also, and it works. But it doesn't work so well when you are trying to serve for a volleyball game. We brought them more balls than any other school, and I'm glad we did. The teachers were almost in tears over the gift.

On South Coast, we spent our time in the village of Tiwi gathering stories. We brought an outline and asked the kids in grade four and grade eight to share their stories with us, stories of what life was like before having the opportunity to go to the school, and after. We asked them about their goals, ambitions, and families. We also asked them about what, if any, relationship they might have with Christ. We hope someday we can find someone with video savyness willing to come along on a trip so we can capture some of these stories and share them directly with people on Facebook and on our website. But for now some of these stories are shared in Chapter 9.

## HELPING OTHERS!

There was some follow up work to do for some other people who are trying to build a rescue center in Vipingo. A rescue center is similar to an orphanage, but kids would come to rescue centers in emergency situations. Whereas at orphanages, children usually come in at birth or around birth. Rescue center kids come in at all different ages and stages of childhood because of abuse at home, death of parents, etc. We've had various meetings with government officials along with social workers, George and Paul, from Vipingo. We've also had some meetings with architects on the layout of the property and building. This got things moving along nicely.

It seems ironic to be a part of this project, though a very small part. The funny thing is - this was always my dream. If I could do anything I wanted to do, I would so LOVE to build an orphanage and hang out with the little kids whenever I came. That would be my dream. God has shifted that dream just a little bit to make it fall in line with His plans for me. So now --hopefully soon-- I will be able to come over and hang out with little itty-bitty babies and their moms who need support and encouragement - even better!

## GIRL TIMES!!!

We were able to meet with the women in Vipingo for women's Bible study twice. We were able to join with them as Nicole did a Bible study with them and also pray with them.

We were only able to see Bomani on the last Tuesday we were in Kenya. This was because the mother of Emily, one of the teachers, had just passed away. It was nice to see her and be able to comfort her after a such a tough trip across country to bury her mom. While we were there, Suzette got a chance to see the child she prays for and sponsors through Fox River.

We also got a chance to catch up and encourage the young mom of the tiny baby we saw at the Fox River farm on the last trip. This was the case where the young mom had been abused by her dad resulting in the pregnancy. The baby looked so healthy and was laughing and engaging with us. The mom, after a while, warmed up to us, and started smiling a little bit, and engaging with Jayne Claire. You could see how proud she was of her little baby girl. I hope we left her encouraged. Her story keeps me moving on the Pregnancy Crisis Center.

## NEXT STEPS - PREGNANCY CENTER

For the pregnancy center we meet with seven different hotels asking for donations of supplies to get the center started. We also meet with some government officials on some aspects of the work. Thanks to two generous donations right before we left, we were able to leave the funds with Rashid to work on getting a carpenter to build a bunk bed and two cribs with drawers underneath for storage.

Also regarding the pregnancy center, we visited the property with Allan, the Pastor who has helped us start all this work. He sent his architect to look at the building for his advice. The architect indicated that he was concerned about adding floors to the existing structure because it had been sitting exposed for so many years. He didn't feel the lower level could handle the weight of a second floor at this point.

This was devastating news! Adding additional floors had been our plan all along. In addition, the news came on the last full day we were visiting, and JJ was at the retreat, so there wasn't any time to talk it through in person. We didn't have a lot of time to get more people over there for second opinions either. After some prayer we thought we could build another structure on the back of the lot, but we had no time to discuss this as a team before we left. This idea would leave the lot very tight with buildings and not much green space at all. It felt like I was leaving with everything up in the air, again.

## TRIP WAS NOT WHAT I EXPECTED

I had lots of tears this trip, which is not unusual for me in Kenya, but this time it was different. Usually my tears come from one of three things.

*One* – having that feeling of actually being the hands and feet of God to someone in need is very overwhelming. This overwhelming feeling is amplified when you see such dire poverty all around you. The need is so great and the consequences of not helping are desperate.

*Second* - the feeling of why would God choose me? I am not good enough for this role at all. Look at the laundry list of bad things I have done in my lifetime. Look at how undeserving I am. Yet He lets me feel like I am His hands and feet to people. That I don't understand, and it overwhelms me with emotion when He uses me.

*Third* – I get overwhelmed by tears when I see people at the village who don't even have enough to eat, who have children who are very sick, and are maybe even very sick themselves, yet they are joyful, uncomplaining, loving, and grateful. What really breaks me, is that despite their substantial lack, I see them giving out of what they do have. Compared to what we see in the US and other parts of the Western world, here it seems there is so little to be grateful for that there is no reason to be giving. They should be holding on to all they have just to stay alive and feed themselves and their family, yet they don't, they give. And you know what – they are 100% happier, more joyful, and more content than those of us who live a Western lifestyle will ever be.

This brings me tears of joy for them, and tears of pity for "my" half of the world, wondering if most of us will ever get it. Joy and gratitude will not expand as our house, cars, electronic gadgets and pocketbooks expand. Our joy and gratitude will only expand as we give what we have away and let God use us to make this world a better place. We need to do this in whatever way He calls us, and wherever He calls us to do it. The Kenyans are such a great example of this lifestyle and I am so grateful for the opportunity I've had to witness it first-hand. My hope is that this book might be used by God to help facilitate this process for you.

## THIS TRIP WAS DIFFERENT

I was in tears both internally and externally for other reasons this trip. There were frustrations over things not going as planned, and in some cases moving backwards. Struggles with personality differences arose a few times. There was also sadness over another reminder that our lives can be very short. I was physically very sick –four or five days of not being able to keep anything in my stomach -- and canker sores that made it impossible to eat. Then there is always the financial stress of the trip. Do we have enough? Keeping everything organized and itemized. Making sure we are not over-spending in some areas. Hoping we have all that we need.

In addition to the mission project finances, there is always a dilemma when starting any venture -- what comes first, the chicken or the egg? Do we raise all the funds first and then start the project, or do we slowly but surely start the project and then pray the funds come? Where do we go for the funds? What if they don't come? Then we have pregnant girls and babies living with us and no money to feed or take care of them. What then?

Those are thoughts that I live with every day. There are definitely days I would like to give up, put this all behind me and say, "look at how simple and stress-free life would be." I could focus on my kids and my job and come home and that would be all. How simple would that be? But then, the pictures fill my mind of the girls out on the street, desperate, hungry, tired, and alone. Pregnant with nowhere to go and no one to help, kicked out of school and home, all alone. Then "she" pops in my head and I know there's no way I can give up. These girls did not ask for this situation and now that I know about their plight, I can't walk away and leave them desperate and abandoned. I can't solve the problem, but I can do my part.

## SUDDEN TRAGEDY

Our goal on this trip was to get as much done as physically possible to get the pregnancy center ready to open. Because of some very serious and deeply saddening circumstances, it was not possible to accomplish everything I had hoped for. God used this situation to teach me several lessons about myself and about Him.

A few days into our trip, a beloved family member of Crossroads Fellowship, Ebba (Caroline), who was well known by the Fox River family for all her work on the last medical mission trip in February 2013, passed away unexpectedly. She handled all the church's administrative duties while another secretary was out on maternity leave. She was also vital in her role for the church in "Driven 4 Him", the middle and high school ministries, and in other areas.

We saw her in passing on Saturday morning at the church. On Monday afternoon, after a Zumba workout, this 32-year-old mom of a four-year-old girl and wife to my dear friend Robert passed away. It was so sudden and such a shock. It brought more fear to people who had already just experienced the terror attack losses and instability in their country.

Ebba made a huge difference everyday in her life and it was shining bright at all the services held in her honor even before the funeral. She certainly did not wait to make a difference in her world. She was a huge part of the church and community through so many different activities, even with a young child at home, including mentoring newly married girls and women, in addition to all the leaderships roles she had at church. She was involved in so much, and was such a great example of not waiting to make a difference.

The father of my children passed away very unexpectedly in 2007. My kids were ten and seven at the time. So I know a little about how it feels to be left behind to deal with the children's response to death at the same time as dealing with your own responses. It is especially hard when the person who passes away is young. I think it adds another level of facing our own mortality no matter the age. I was glad to be able to share a little bit with Robert before we left, and on Facebook after I was back in the US. I pray that Robert and Iman will continue to carry on Ebba's amazing example.

Another issue was our lack of time together to work as a board for the pregnancy center. Mbeyu had a lot to do to help with Iman and the church for Ebba's funeral. Mbeyu and Ebba were best friends. They had both been married quite awhile without having kids and both got pregnant at the same time. This was devastating for her and she needed to keep things together for Iman while Robert was getting everything ready.

While we were there, Jane Jilani had a two week long retreat for her ministerial duties, so we didn't have more than probably two or three hours together. The short time we did have together left me questioning what we were doing there.

We had some really important details to work through on the next steps of the ministry. Chicken and the egg type discussions - what comes first a paid employee or funding the buildings and other needs? We had someone who wished to work for the organization in Kenya. We had given her a trial period with certain expectations. Those expectations where claimed to have been met. There was a specific procedure that was supposed to be followed to prove the conditions were met, and that procedure was not followed. That left the person in a difficult financial position. Not an easy conversation at all, but in the end we all agreed. I donated from my own funds to fix the immediate financial position and we decided no paid employees would be hired until later in the process.

Then of course there was the issue of the building and it's safety which came up right as I was leaving. So that was difficult too.

I was also sick and tired. I was physically sick and tired as well as spiritually and emotionally. I was to the point of no energy on day three and four of the illness. I needed extra sleep to maintain even that level of energy.

In addition to that, all the stresses in Kenya, the coming and going so quickly from home, and the fact that we had two huge fund raising projects that were weighing on my mind. With all of this, my rough edges were starting to show in my interactions with people and in my own thoughts. God was showing me in so many ways so many things that were still in my heart that need to be changed. At the time I was not much in the "mood" to listen.

These are a few of the major things God showed me on this trip. I wonder how many of these you can relate with.

## GOD'S LESSONS FOR ME ON THIS TRIP

### 1. Priorities. What's the real point of all this?

What is the real point of these trips to Kenya? What is the real priority in life anywhere?

Is it to get things done? I'd like to think that it is. Get it done and check it off the list. This is clean, easy to judge, and gives a sense of accomplishment.

All good things. Very black and white, and easy to see. But God is showing me this is not what this life is all about.

Our real priority should be: to love God and then love anyone God puts around me to love. It doesn't get much simpler than that. This helps keep the focus. But man is it difficult! I don't always want to love the people in front of me. Sometimes I don't know how to love the people in front of me. But through Him I will be able to love by keeping the focus on being loving, and keep the focus off myself and what I think or want.

I have to focus on being and not doing. Busyness and being very task oriented are very difficult areas for me. Our society likes and encourages it so much. Work harder and longer. It's all worth it.

But I'm finding that tasks too often steal away my real focus. If I just get this done, then I can love someone else by encouraging them or sitting down with them or sending them a note or giving them a call. But the real focus should always be on the people, not the tasks. It's hard for me because I can control the tasks. Tasks don't hurt me with an email or an angry word. Not only that, I can get reward out of a task, a sense of accomplishment, the full day was not totally "wasted", this or that was accomplished. But the real point of being here is about relationships. Relationship number one with God for leading and guidance, and then with others, all others that God puts in our path.

The examples on this trip are too numerous to count. One might be how we took the time to comfort Robert and other members at Crossroads Fellowship in anyway we could, even if that wasn't the original plan. It was necessary to change our plans around because of a death in a teacher's family. When it comes down to it, this is allowing God to dictate the schedule, not my written piece of paper I typed up prior to coming to Kenya. Go with the flow and be fully in the moment not thinking about what might happen next.

### 2. Guard your heart.

No matter what is going on around me, God has me where He has me and I need to keep focused on Him and what He has in store, not on what other people are doing or not doing. It is too easy to get distracted because of tiredness, overworking my mind, or other people's actions. But God calls us to stay focused on our mission with Him, not His mission with anyone else.

Not guarding your heart will lead to bitterness and resentment. If we allow other people to become our focus, we can become bitter and angry. We have to stay focused on Him and follow His lead. As Pastor Guy always preaches, "We can be bitter, or we can be better, but we cannot be both. We have to decide which one is more important to us." Most of us decide this unconsciously and stay in bitterness, but if we are conscious about it, we can overcome bitterness and move into betterness. At first, it is a moment to moment decision and as we start making the right decisions on what to focus on, it becomes easier and easier.

Some examples on this trip were interactions with travel-mates, like Colton not engaging at some of our stops or some of the personality differences with others. At first I wanted to pass judgment and be bitter over these situations. But then a great friend on Facebook reminded me - focus on the mission - not the distractions. Focus on God and what He is asking of me and not what I think other people should or shouldn't be doing.

### 3. God's timing.

In our work on most trips, I feel like we are running in circles, or even worse, going backwards. For example, if we have to do A through Z to get the pregnancy center up and running, I feel like I am at point M and when I leave we are way back at point C. It feels like we are going backwards.

I'm grateful no money had been wasted, but time becomes a great self-imposed pressure to me. First and most importantly, I know there are girls struggling greatly NOW. It is hard for me to be patient. Second, donors and sponsors are donating their money to make a difference, yet details of the plan keep changing.

What I need to do is pray for the current girls and just do what God is calling me to do at the time He is calling me to do it. I can do no more and I am not called to do any more. But on the other hand, I cannot do any less if He is calling me to do something. I need to do it immediately, not when I get around to it. This is a constant balancing act I have to be careful of. I don't want to move too fast, but I am fearful of moving too slow. Waiting on God's timing is very difficult for me.

**4. Focus.**

This one overlaps a little bit with guarding your heart, but it is also different. I cannot let my disappointment over situations or personality differences pull my focus away from following what God is asking me to do. Life stays joyful and content when I keep my focus on God and not let it get distracted by circumstances or other people's behavior.

I have a lot of different examples of this. One simple example from this trip was the work we were doing in helping another group get started on building a rescue center on the property in Vipingo. There were various village and community meetings and other administrative meetings that were necessary which I conducted.

These led to opportunities for further meetings in development of their project. It was hard to say no to these because I always want to help and learn more. These meetings would have been fun and informative and I would have enjoyed them. But I needed to stay focused on the purpose of the trip, which was to do whatever it takes to help the pregnancy center move forward. It was hard for me to say no, and stay focused. I can't always be a people pleaser or satisfy my urge to learn more and more.

**5. Slow Down/Rest = Better Communication**

I was very sick on this trip. On most trips I have an evening or two, or maybe a day that I'm not feeling great. This trip was really tough. I was unable to eat anything (or keep it down) for four or five days. I didn't even have the energy to smile toward the end. We still covered everything on our itinerary, but I stepped back and allowed others take the lead, which was good. I was glad to get my energy back when I did, but it was a good lesson in slowing down and resting. I do too much! My word for the next year is REST which I would be studying and focusing on. I needed it!

More rest, less busy = better communication. Because I have been so over-stretched in commitments lately, I am finding quite a few problems in communication. I'm rushing things, which leads to problems in emails, texting, and phone conversations. I need to learn to delegate and ask for help. If I don't get the help, then the project doesn't get done and I need to be okay with that as part of God's plan. I need to take the time to fully explain things to whoever I am working with to avoid communication problems later.

Slowing down does so much good for me and my physical and emotional state, which also improves the ministry.

### 6. People pleasing vs. taking authority.

I am not the type of person who likes to tell people what to do and when to do it, unless you're my child or my athlete. I like to hear everyone's ideas and do everything possible to fit all those ideas into what we are doing. That is not a bad thing, but there does come a time when circumstances dictate that things will have to be moved, and/or let go of completely. I need to stand up, take charge, and not feel guilty about it.

I also need to be careful not to let other people's wants dictate what the mission does. Again, it is not a bad thing to fit in all we can given the interests of a group, but there are times due to safety, situations with people in Kenya, or other things, that I will not be able to "please everyone". I need to be okay with that. I need to put my foot down politely and in love for everyone involved; the Kenyans, Americans, and the mission in general. I need to be okay with the fact that someone may be disappointed, and even possibly angry.

The Bible in Luke 12:48 says with great blessing comes great responsibility. I like the blessing but I would rather not have to discipline or disappoint people. I need to assume the authority when needed.

### OTHER TAKEAWAYS FROM THIS TRIP

Colton did a great job helping us organize back at the house, getting things ready, and really enjoyed the beach time we had in South Coast. He was not as engaged in our activities in the schools and orphanages as I would have liked him to be, but we did get closer as we spent the two weeks together.

On the way home we had an overnight layover in Amsterdam. It was cool to hop on the bus and see the whole city just Colton and I. We stopped at a place for a burger at the end of the bus line and then hopped back on to see the city again at sunset. Biggest takeaway from Amsterdam was the hundreds of bicycles. The way the city was laid out more for bikes than motor vehicles was mind boggling.

Suzette was a great addition in a lot of ways. Her work with Jayne Claire in approaching seven different hotels on the coast for donations of dishes, plates, and other household items, as well as for financial support, was un- paralleled. She was the perfect person for the job. This was her first trip and she jumped right in.

For me the biggest takeaway was everything I outlined above, but in gen- eral - what is the purpose of these trips? What was the best use of our time? What is the goal? On this trip I thought the goal was to do leg work to get the pregnancy center one step closer to reality. But God had other plans and showed me the real purpose. To build relationships and help - emotionally, spiritually, financially, intellectually - however I can, wherever it's needed. He will bring the situations to me - I don't have to pre-plan everything. But I do have to be in the moment and forget about my to-do list.

## COMING HOME

Upon return, the run/walk was just a few days away. My goal this year was to double entries from 50 to 100. That goal was not met. About 75 people registered for the event, but we met with an even better success. We doubled our profits without doubling our entries. It is a better success because every entry costs us in food, water, and T-shirts, so double our entrants does not necessarily mean doubling our profits. I have to watch how I set goals in the future! God has so much more for us than we ever could think to ask for.

The profits from the run/walk get split between different areas. Some of the profits go directly to Peter and Selpher's Baby Life Rescue Orphanage and some go toward the pregnancy center. I am hoping that we can expand the run to other cities, even if it is by virtual run format!

Special thanks to Maria Frederick and Olga Ceballos. They secured an interview with Jane Ford and the local New Berlin Now newspaper. She ended up doing three separate articles. One on the run/walk for African Orphans, kind of like a save-the-date. Then the week of the event she did a story about my book, my involvement with the centers in Kenya, as well as about the run. This was a big step for us! Our first publicity other than social media!

## SHOES AND SPEAKING - GREAT COMBINATION

I have been receiving invitations for more and more speaking engagements lately. Most of the speaking stems from the shoe drive. In Lake Geneva, a Mothers of Preschoolers (MOPS) Group invited me to their meeting to speak about life in Kenya and how the shoes will make a difference. They had been collecting shoes for a few weeks, and we had a lot of bags of shoes to bring home. People from the group have been calling me and we have set up times to pick up even more shoes!

St. Elizabeth Ann Seton, a church here in New Berlin, was having a rummage in July. I ride by their church all the time, so I thought I would reach out and ask them for their left over shoes (I do that at a lot of rummages these days). I got in touch with the person in charge of the rummage and they said not to wait till the rummage was over, but to come at 2:00p.m. and we could take all the shoes that were there. When we came, the shoes filled up the entire back of my car!

From touching base on the shoes, they heard about our work in Kenya. Every November, they have a weekend retreat for their high school kids on poverty awareness. They stay overnight on Saturday outside in cardboard boxes, and have a few guest speakers talk on various topics related to poverty. This year, I was asked if I could come and speak and give a global perspective on poverty. The kids were fully engaged and attentive, especially for so early on a Sunday morning.

At that retreat there were a few homeschooled children. They have home-school programs on Fridays at a church in Brookfield. Students come together for gym and speech classes, and some other projects. They asked if I could come speak to their high-school groups about Kenya and life in Kenya. The visual part of the presentation did not go as planned, but we had a good time doing scavenger hunts through the first book, and various Kenya scrapbooks I have created and printed over the years. The kids also collected some baby clothes, school supplies, and shoes.

I so love sharing God's workings through speaking. It re-energizes and reminds me again of how much I have to be thankful for.

## CRAFTS, BAGS, JEWELRY AND SPEAKING

I had a little display, as I always do when I speak, of a few Kenyan items to bring a little feeling of Africa to the room. I use the items we sell at the craft fairs for this purpose, but I just bring a few things. After the group presentation, the moms and kids were looking at the scrapbooks and the items (necklaces and a few bags). It was a week or two before Christmas. Needless to say, I sold every item I brought with me that day and they invited me back the next week to have the whole spread out for sale to all the kids and parents. Between that and a few dear Kenyan-American friends Christmas shopping, I sold almost every item we brought back from Kenya on all three trips this year! All of the funds from the sales go directly back to Kenya to build the Pregnancy Crisis Center.

## IT'S NOT ALWAYS EASY AND NOT ALWAYS CLEAR

It was about this time that life was losing its joy for me. Everything seemed to be a struggle. Lots of normally easy relationships were difficult. The only relationships that were not much of a problem were with my kids and husband, and the funny part is, those relationships tend to be stumbling blocks for me.

I'm not sure why joy felt distant. I guess it's a combination of things. God showing me that I am too busy which leads to that feeling of burnout. Then the devil jumping into my thoughts and mind along with multiple attacks from different areas of my life all trying to pull me down.

I found myself struggling with people wanting to put me on a pedestal, wanting to make me out as someone so different than everyone else. In the process they were all excepting perfection from me. But I am just a normal person who makes mistakes with my kids, my mouth, and my ideas all the time. I am no different than anyone reading this book. The stories you read about here are a result of God working, not me. These stories show an example of how God can work through you if you are willing to risk letting Him. But I do not deserve a pedestal - only Jesus does.

Another area of struggle for me is confusion. Most of my confusion revolves around what I should be doing and what I shouldn't be doing. For example, craft sales bring in most of the income for the pregnancy center right now. I feel like God is pulling me away from doing all the work myself. He wants me to focus more on other parts of the organization of Operation Give Hope.

This leads to confusion for me because these are actually money-making ventures for us. The things I feel He is leading me to are not direct money-making ventures. We cannot do what we do without money, so I struggle in letting this activity go. I know God CAN produce funds in whatever way he pleases, but I guess I am struggling with the HOW.

In addition to that confusion, at our board meeting last year, getting office space for Operation Give Hope was discussed. At a craft fair this year we found very inexpensive office space which led me to make a few calls. I feel like we have found some really good office space but I'm not sure what God wants in this area. The space is a one-of-a-kind type space. We need a space that has traffic and windows for a store, but also works well as an office.

I found one that would be perfect in Hales Corners right by the post office, but I'm afraid to jump. First, we have zero in overhead expenses right now, and I like that. All our funds go directly to the kids. Leasing an office would mean monthly payments for rent, heat, WIFI, etc.. Second, I know God is calling me to REST. "Rest" is the word God has me working on for 2014. I'm not sure how jumping into an office space would lead to more rest. Knowing my personality, I would want the store open every possible minute to make it worth the rent and other expenses we are paying. So this is very confusing for me.

## FINDING ANSWERS

I know I need to rely more on God for the answers. I'm grateful I know that much. For most of my life I thought I had to rely on reading the right book, meeting the right person, doing the right thing, or watching the right shows to find answers for my life. At least I know where to turn and Who to trust, and that my answers will come from there.

Relying less on myself is difficult, and that is where most of these struggles are coming from. I don't always like it, but for all of this to work, I have to follow His lead, not mine. I have to slow down, pray, and listen for the next steps. I have to rely on Him for guidance, not my own knowledge. Stay tuned and we will see where God takes all of this from here.

## WHAT IS NEXT FOR YOU?

Enough about me and Kenya for now. Let's hear from the Kenyan kids themselves and then what about you? What is your first "yes" to God? What is your next "yes" to God? Let's take some time to find out together.

*Chapter 9*

# Stories from Kenya

I want to introduce you to one of our grade eight classes. Enjoy their stories!

## ALI TIMA TUNZA

Ali Tima Tunza was born on August 28, 1999, and she is in the 8th grade. This 14-year-old lives in Tiwi village with her mom, dad, and her two siblings. Her sister Halima Ali Tunza goes to Matuga Girls High School and her brother Mohamed Ali goes to Tiwi Redeemed School. Every day Ali leaves at 6 am to get to school, which is 1 kilometer away. Her favorite subject is math because she enjoys making calculations. She would like to attend university because she dreams of becoming a doctor one day. She wants to make sure the sick are well treated. Her favorite aspect of school is learning about Jesus every Friday, and she loves going to church and being with her parents. Ali Tima wishes one day to change her current living status. After being asked how her life was like before going to this school, she responded that her life was worse because she did not know how to read and write, and because she did not know about Jesus and God. She believes that by learning about the Christian faith at her school, she has become fearful before the eyes of God. This, according to Ali, has made her special and made her certain that she is going to heaven. Ali Tima is a disciplined girl who can be a great person in the future.

## MGANGA SAMUEL JEEWA

Mganga Samuel Jeewa is a 13-year-old born on February 29, 2000, who lives at Tiwi Sport with his mom, dad, aunt, and siblings. His siblings Ronald and Christine attend Tiwi Baptist Academy, while Elizabeth attends New MRB River Academy. He has to walk 1 kilometer to get to school, so he needs to leave by 5:30 am to get to school on time. Although Samuel's favorite subject is math, he would like to be a singer when he grows up, because he is very passionate about singing. In fact, since the 7th grade he has always recorded himself singing songs, especially those that gave great meaning to him. He hopes to one day go to university. What Samuel likes best about his current school is that the teachers are confident and they help him understand various topics. According to him, before attending this school, his life was "boring and bad". He is glad that he is able to obtain so much knowledge from this school. He has learned from school that Jesus has saved us from our sins, that He died and went to heaven, and that He is now seated at the right hand of God. Samuel believes that he is going to heaven because he believes in Jesus and because Jesus has forgiven his sins. Additionally, he wants to sings songs that will make God and Jesus happy, so he will be "the greatest singer on earth." Samuel appreciates how his teachers and classmates constantly encourage him to continue pursuing his passion. He hopes to one day make a CD of his music, but cannot do so currently because he does not have enough money.

## MWAMBAWA SALIM

Mwambawa Salim is 15 years old and is in the 8th grade. His sibling Fauz attends Christina Academy, and Juma attends Shimba Hills High School. He lives with his father 4 kilometers away from school. Because of this far distance from school, Mwambawa must leave at 5:00 to get to school in the morning. His favorite subject is English, and he would like to be a journalist because he wants to collect information and inform. The favorite part of his life is changing other people's behavior. However, like many of the other students, Mwambawa hopes to change his living standard one day. Before he got to this school, he believed that life was too difficult for him. Now that he attends this school, he feels that he has gotten to know the right religion and has accepted Jesus as his Savior. One thing that makes him special is that he is the best football player in his village and at school. The child wrote a tribute to his teacher, Mr. Fred:

"Mr. Fred is his name. A man of integrity who came full of wisdom and strong personality. Leading in peace, love and unity, wisely as he judged through hills and valleys, have we trudged, overcoming hardships, through his mighty leadership. Oh! Lord bless our magnificent headmaster. Give him health in body and sober mind, to guide with principles, unite us for success as our motto goes "A step in the right direction".

## BERHARD KAMUU JOHN

Berhard Kamuu John is a focused student born on July 27, 1997. He lives in the village of Moweni with his dad, brother, and sister. His brother Peter also attends Tiwi Baptist Academy, while his sister Cecilia attends Matuaa High School. He lives 1 kilometer away from school, and leaves home at 6:00 am to get to school on time. His favorite subject is science, because he enjoys learning about the environment. When he grows up, he wants to be a pilot because he wants the lives of people to be safe in his hands. What he likes best about his school is that it teaches Christian values everyday and every hour. In his free time, he enjoys swimming and riding. Berhard wishes that he could change a part of his life by helping his family and other people in his country. He believes that before attending this school, his life was dark because he did not know God and he did not participate in certain activities that he currently participates in. Now that he attends this school, he can do many activities on his own such as reading and writing. Berhard believes that what makes him special is that he is wonderfully and fearfully made by God.

## ABDALLAH MARIAM MWAKWAMBALLA

Abdallah Mariam Mwakwamballa is a 15-year-old living in Tiwi village with her mom, dad, and two siblings. Binti attends Skuda Academy, and Tuma goes to Kenyatta High School. Every day she leaves home at 6:00 am and walks 1 kilometer to school. She enjoys math as a subject because to her it is easy to understand. When she grows up, she dreams of being an advocate so she can reduce the rate of corruption. In order to become an advocate, she understands that she needs to acquire a masters degree. Her favorite part about school is the sports it offers. When asked what part of her life she would like to change, she responded that she does not have the power to change her life but she trusts God would mold her to be a better person before His eyes. Before attending this school, Mariam found her studies quite difficult, and she is glad that she can now read and understand. She is a hardworking and well-rounded young girl who is prepared for future leadership.

## MWASEMA MAIMUNA

15-year-old Mwasema Maimuna lives in Mkoyo village with both of her parents, one kilometer away from school. Her siblings Misaim Ali attends Tiwi B. Academy and Rayyan Ali attends Bright Star school. She enjoys math because to her it is easy to calculate, and she aspires to one day become a doctor. Her dream to obtain a medical degree is deeply rooted in her desire to help all people worldwide and to give service to patients. Mwasema's favorite part of her life is learning. When we asked her what part of her life she wishes she could make different, she replied, "I don't have the power to change my life but I trust that God transforms people. I wish God to mold me to be a better and useful vessel before his eyes." Before going to this school, she found life very difficult and she is grateful that this school has made her better able to work out any sum. She is also glad that she has learned about God and Jesus and how she was wonderfully and fearfully made. Mwasema Maimuna is a focused young girl who is academically skilled and full of potential.

## MWANAMWALI KESI

Mwanamwali Kesi was born in June 1998 and lives in Somoni village. She lives with her mom, dad, and sisters, who go to Mt. Sinai School. Every morning, she leaves home at 6:00 am and rides 6 kilometers to get to school. Her favorite subjects are math and science because she finds them easy to work out. One day she hopes to earn a P.H.D. and become a doctor because she would like to help those who are suffering. Mwanamwali loves the sports and games offered at her school, and her favorite part of life is playing with her pupils. Before attending this school, she believed that her life was in hell because she had not yet given her life to Jesus Christ. Since she came to this school, she has opened her heart to Jesus Christ, and her life is now like, in her words, "a shining moon." Although she is glad that her life changed for the better after coming to this school, she hopes to also change her village. She would like to construct tarmac roads. Mwanamwali is a very determined girl who heeds instructions and corrections.

## HAMINI MWIANAIDI GATTANA

Hamini Mwianaidi Gattana lives in Tiwi village with both of her parents. Her siblings Sikukuu, Momo, and Salama attend Bright Star Academy, Tiwi Baptist School, and Kwale Girls School, respectively. Hamini is 15 years old and is in the 8th grade. She leaves home at 6:00 am every day and rides 1 km to get to school. She loves science as a subject because to her it is interesting and requires a lot of reasoning. This student dreams of one day becoming a lawyer, because she wants to make sure justice is done to all. Her under-standing of being a lawyer is that you find evidence about your client to win cases. She loves that her school offers games that improve every student's different talents. As a helpful and hardworking girl, Hamini's favorite part of life is "helping the aged and keeping the environment clean." She hopes one day to change her village into a big city with a great transportation system and communication network. As a strong believer of Christ, this pupil un-derstands that what makes her special is that she was made in the image and likeness of God, and that Jesus died for her sins.

## HADIJA HASSAN

Hadija Hassan is an ambitious student born on March 15, 1999. In Tiwi Mobriva, she lives with her mom, dad, and brother, who attends Waa Boys High School. Every morning, she departs from home at 6:00 and walks 2 kilometers to school. Because science is her favorite subject, she would like to be a doctor when she grows up. She dreams of earning a masters degree in order to treat people who are sick or injured. as well as help people in her community. Hadija believes that before attending this school, her life was difficult and dark because she did not know about God. However, although she is grateful that her life has improved, she still prays to God to better her life in different ways. This 14-year-old loves playing games offered at her school, and believes that the most important part of her life is learning. Overall, Hadija is a hardworking, determined, and focused pupil.

## JUMA TATU TEMO

Juma Tatu Temo is 14 years old and was born on October 4. She lives in the Sport Area with her mom and dad. She has four siblings. The schools they attend include Tiwi B. Academy, O.R. Babler, Thaufic, and U.K.P. Each morning, she leaves her house at 5:40 and walks to school. Her favorite subject is math because she enjoys computing math problems. When she grows up, she would love to be a doctor and treat the sick, especially those who are poor. She understands that she will have to attend university to achieve this goal. Juma's favorite aspect of her current school is the beautiful environment as well as the determination of her peers. Her favorite part of life is spending time with her classmates and friends. Despite loving her school and friends, she still desires some change in her life. She wishes to change her living status. Overall, this school has helped this student learn to better associate with others, and taught her about God and Jesus. In fact, she has learned that what makes her special is that she is wonderfully and fearfully made. Juma is a determined girl who dreams of brightening her future through education. She also has a very positive attitude.

## MARSHA SANITA KIFAW

8th grader Marsha Sanita Kifaw was born on February 12, 1998. She lives in Maweni with both of her parents. Her siblings Amani and Sifa both attend Tiwi B. Academy. She must walk 1 kilometer to get to school, so she leaves home at 6:00 am. Her favorite subject is math because she feels that it makes her mind fresh. One day Marsha hopes to be a doctor. Her understanding of the tasks doctors must complete include waking up early to go and treat the sick and take care of them. After being asked what she loves best about her current school, she responded that she liked how the teachers teach them about God and the beautiful environment they live in. Marsha, like most of the other pupils, wishes she could change her living status. However, she appreciates life and especially loves to read the Bible. She feels that before attending this school, her life was terrifying because she did not know how to read and write, and she did not know about God. This school has taught her that Jesus is the only way to heaven and that God created her in His own likeness and image. Although this young girl is full of potential, she could do better in academics.

## NYADZYE BEAUTY MWANGATA

Nyadzye Beauty Mwangata is a 15-year-old girl who was raised in a Christian family. She lives in the Sport area with her parents and siblings. Her sister Bentia and brother Brian both attend Tiwi B. Academy. She leaves home at 6:00 am and walks 1 kilometer to school each day. Her favorite subject is science because she likes how it teaches her more about behavior. Nyadzye's academic preferences reflect what she wants to be when she grows up: a nurse. To be specific, she dreams of attending university so she can learn to treat and cure people in hospitals. What she likes best about school is the great teaching methods. What she likes best about life is when she is with her teachers and classmates. Although Nyadzye wishes she could make different her living status and family, she is grateful that she has learned from school to read, write, and to forgive others. This school has also further taught her about Christianity, specifically, that Jesus Christ is her personal Savior and is the only way to heaven. Despite being a straightforward and disciplined student, she needs encouragement and prayers.

## RASHID MSOMALI MWAKIROHO

Born on May 30, Rashid Msomali Mwakiroho is a 16-year-old girl living in Kirudi village. She lives with her mom, dad, and three siblings. Sudi attends Kwale High, Athuman attends Tiwi Primary, and Fatuma attends Tiwi B. Academy. Like many of her classmates, she lives 1 kilometer away and must leave at 6:00 am to get to school on time. Msomali's favorite subject is mathematics because she loves dealing with numbers. One day she hopes to complete university and become a doctor, so she can cure the sick every day. School is a very important part of her life. Not only is her favorite part of life school, she also believes that this school has "made [her] achieve [her] goals." Before she got to this school, her life was difficult, and she could not imagine overcoming this difficulty. Msomali feels that what makes her special is her knowledge as well as her belief that God and Jesus is her shining light who will save her. This pupil is very polite and has great potential to excel.

## HAMISI YUMUS MOHAMMED

Hamisi Yumus Mohammed is 14 years old and lives in Mkoyo village with his mom, brother, and sister. His sibling, Ridhiami Mohammed, attends Tiwi B., while his other sibling, Rayyam Kwale, attends Methodi School. His favorite subject is English because it is the official language and because he dreams of becoming a journalist when he is older. As a journalist, he would collect information and inform Kenyans what is going on in Kenya and all over the country. Hamisi hopes to achieve this goal by obtaining a P.H.D. His favorite aspect of life is when he preaches to his fellow pupils about Jesus Christ, the son of God. Before attending this school, his life was tough for many reasons. He could not pronounce words well, he often had to go to school hungry and with a torn uniform, and he had no idea about Jesus Christ. Now that he is in this school, he can get food every day and he believes in Jesus Christ as his Savior. This student believes what makes him special is that he is the best basketball player in his school and village and that he is the captain of the basketball team. Overall, he is a disciplined, well behaved boy who is always guided by this principle: cleanliness is next to Godliness. He's hardworking and self driven!

## MOHAMMED RNGADHAN MWANASITI

Mohammed Rngadhan Mwanasiti is a young boy born on March 15, 1998. This 8th grader lives in Kibarani with his mom, dad, and relatives. His sibling Juma also attends Tiwi Baptist Academy. Every day he leaves home at 6:00 and rides to school. He enjoys mathematics a lot because it makes his mind busy. When he grows up, he dreams of being a pilot, because he believes that being a pilot would help his parents and others. He delights in the fact that his school continues with the same spirit of helping every pupil, and his favorite part of life is when he is worshipping God. When we asked him what he would like to change in his life, he humbly replied that he does not want to change any part of his life, but he prays to God to guide him in the right path in his lifetime. Before he got to this school, Mohammed faced many challenges, so he is very glad that his new school has given him a vision of what he can be in the future. The student believes that what makes him special is his behavior, his faith, and his acceptance as Jesus Christ as his Savior. Mohammed is a very focused pupil, but needs close attention and prayers.

## SALIM GAPHONZE JUMA

Salim Gaphonze Juma lives in Tiwi village with both of his parents. The 15-year-old has two brothers: Salim, who attends Kenya TTA High School, and Omar, who attends Kirudi Primary School. Each morning, he leaves home at 5:30 am and walks 15 miles to school. Because he likes calculation, his favorite subject is mathematics. When he grows up, he wants to be a pilot because to him it would be interesting to travel to different parts of the world. What he likes best about his school is how it offers games and preaches the word of God. Salim's favorite part of life is when he guides young kids and plays with them. He hopes he can change his attitude and one day develop his family and community. Before getting to this school, life was very hard for this pupil. He could not read and pronounce words well, and he often went to school hungry. Now that he attends this school, Salim can read and write proficiently, and has teachers who are very committed to their work. Salim is a hardworking young boy who is always appreciative. He is also the head boy at his school.

## BARAZA JAPHETH MWANGOME

Baraza Japheth Mwangome is a hardworking, determined, and self-driven boy living in Tiwi with his father. The 8th grader was raised in a Christian home, and has a great passion for praise and worship. He has three siblings, two of whom attend Kirudi Primary, and the other attends Kaya Tiwi High School. To get to school, he has to leave at 6:00 am and walk 2 kilometers to school. His favorite subject is English because it will help him become a lawyer. As a lawyer, he hopes to ensure that justice prevails in the courts. He understands that a lawyer's responsibilities include trying to help his or her client win a case, and that he must earn a P.H.D. in law to become a lawyer. Baraza appreciates that his school encourages its pupils both spiritually and academically. When asked how his life was before getting to this school, he stated, "My life was being controlled by Satan and I did not know that Christ died for my sins." His life is very different now that he attends this school because he is leading a spiritual life and has accepted Jesus as his savior. He understands that Jesus died for his sins on the cross so that he can be saved. This boy is filled with hope, but he needs financial support for his academics. He has great potential of securing a chance to attend a national school.

## ABDALLA BIASKA

Born on April 16, 1997, Abdalla Biaska is a disciplined young girl who lives in Sport Area with her parents. Her sibling Zeinar is currently attending finishing school. Her favorite subject is English because she can speak it fluently. One day Abdalla hopes to be a teacher, because she loves having conversation with children and would like to teach children good morals as well as a variety of subjects. While her favorite part of life is being in school, she hopes she can make different her living status and home environment. This pupil is grateful she gets to attend this school because her life was previously very difficult since she was not performing well and she was not friendly to people. She believes that what makes her special is that God has granted her His grace and she is wonderfully and fearfully made. Because Abdalla is sometimes sickly, she needs our prayers for her good health.

## MWAKESU MEBAKARI MATAO

Mwakesu Mebakari Matao is the school head girl living in Sport Area with her dad and mom. She has four siblings; two attend Tiwi B academy, one attends Murray School, and one attends college. Like many of her fellow pupils, she leaves home at 6:00 am and walks 1 kilometer to school. She likes science because she finds it interesting to learn about the behavior of the natural and physical world based on facts that you can prove. When she grows up, this students dreams of becoming a lawyer, who would advise and represent her people in the court of law and fight for their rights. What she likes best about her current school is its beautiful and studious environment. Mwakesu's favorite part of her life is when she is with her classmates and her best friend. She believes that her life was miserable before attending this school because she had not learned about God and Jesus and did not know how to associate with others. It is her belief that what makes her special is that she has God-fearing parents and that she will achieve her studies in God's grace. This girl is a promising student who is full of potential.

## ESTER KALARA LUVUTSE

Raised in a Christian background, Ester Kalara Luvutse is a 14-year-old who lives in Kirundi village with her parents and siblings. She has four siblings; Curtis attends Dr Aggrey High School, Barvan attends Kwale High School, Ruth attends Bura Girls School, and Dorcas attends Tiwi B. Academy. Her favorite subject is Christian theology, because it teaches her more about Jesus Christ. She hopes to one day become a lawyer in order to fight for the rights of the innocent. Ester appreciates that every pupil at her school is very determined, and she loves to spend time with her classmates and family members. Before attending this school, her life was difficult since she was weak and felt lonely and resentful. Not only has this school taught her about Jesus Christ, it has also taught her to appreciate others. Ester is a focused and God-fearing girl who has a bright future ahead of her. She is aspiring and working to join a national school.

*Chapter 10*

# Overcoming Struggles on the Way to Your Difference in this World

Wow, this last chapter has really been a journey for me! I originally wrote this final chapter at the same time as I wrote the rest of this book, in December 2013, when I had a week off of work. When I re-read that final chapter, it was very similar to the last chapter in the first book. Therefore, if you have not read the final chapter of my first book, I would recommend you read it now.

After writing the first draft of this chapter, I had been working for over a year to come up with something for the end of this book that was different than the first book and make it still have meaning and purpose to apply to our lives. I spent many weekends writing hours every day. I thought it was going well, only to go right back to it again feeling it was nowhere near what it needed to be. Sometimes it was just awful! I had no additional ideas or direction on what to do. I was about to give up on the book altogether, but thanks to the encouragement of friends, it has finally arrived into your hands as you are reading it now.

After much prayer, I finally have everything together. I realized that I was trying to fit different stories from the last few years together to make a high quality final chapter to send you off with. What's changed since then is that God has shown me that it is not about pulling lots of great little tidbits together. His purpose is to use me to share one of His messages. So here we are almost one year later … this is a note from God to you (and me).

I do not consider myself an expert or even a good practitioner of the principles laid out in this chapter, but I feel they are things we need to think about and focus on in order to bring our lives to the next level.

I normally don't speak or write with a lot of Bible verses. Though I read the Bible in personal quiet time, I'm not great at memorizing or knowing where to find things. For this chapter, God just really brought some verses to light, so I'll share them with you in snapshot form. My words alone will not change your life. I am only one example of a what can happen when we allow ourselves to be used by God. It is God's Word in the Bible that changed my life, and will change your life.

I hope the snapshots of a few exciting examples of Biblical characters will be the catalyst to get you back into the Word, or into the Word for the first time. If when you first start reading the Bible it is difficult to understand, keep going. It will become clearer and clearer as you read more and more. So keep at it.

I hope you can use this to make great strides in your life.

## OVERCOMING STRUGGLES

This journey From Lawyer to Missionary has not been easy. I would love to say that once I knew where God was leading and started the journey was smooth sailing, but that is not the truth. There were many times of great joy and satisfaction, like having a conversation with a Kenyan or an American that I would not normally have taken the time to have, seeing a great success in a program or funding source, sitting on the school grounds holding a little one who needs some love that day, watching the kids and adults share with others around them and encouraging teachers and seeing the love they have for their students. Those are great moments. Those are great times. And there are a lot of them.

There also are excruciatingly hurtful, frustrating, and hard times. Times I don't understand. Times where I am attacked personally. Times I am judged harshly by people because I work internationally. Times when I have been misunderstood, pushed away and deeply hurt by Kenyans and Americans. Times when I've wanted to throw in the towel and just be done.

I have intense questions with no satisfying answers. Why do people have to go hungry? Why are people dying for lack of a few dollars to get medical care? There are days when I wonder, why am I doing this? Why try anymore? Sometimes I feel like everyone and everything is against me. I feel overwhelmed and don't know what to do next. Those times come, and they are not easy to work through.

Those times happen working in Kenya and in my life right here in America. How do we dig deep and push past those times? Where do we find the strength? What do we do?

I am the first to admit, I have no idea. The answer is - push into God. But to explain what that means is next to impossible because it is different for all of us. What I can share with you are a few things that have worked for me. Hopefully they will work for you too.

## STEPS TO OVERCOMING STRUGGLES

Here are some guidelines to use when struggling.

## CHANGE YOUR THINKING

**FIRST** – focus on the good, noble, and right things.  Do not allow negative energy a space in your head. Don't let the devil of negative thoughts get a tiny foothold in your mind. If you give a little space, before you know it, negative thoughts will take over more and more and your head will be filled with negative thoughts.

How do we change our focus off the bad and onto the good? Start with taking a step back from the person or situation. We tend to look at people or situations as all or nothing. Things are either all good or all bad. That is rarely the case. Step back a while from the situation and FIND the good, no matter how small or hard it might be.

*For example* – your whole family won't come together for Christmas because two people are not speaking with each other and it is your FAVORITE time of the year. We tend to focus on the fact that we don't get our perfect Christmas. Poor me. I only want my family together at Christmas. Is that so much to ask?

Or we can take a step back and focus on other aspects of the situation. If the whole family doesn't come together on one day, you get to have multiple Christmases. You will have a lot of quality one-on-one time with all the people over a longer period of time instead of intense craziness/busyness with everyone at one time. The negative is still there, yes, but it is not controlling you. You can see the benefit of the situation which diffuses the negative and changes your focus.

**SECOND** - get good counsel. The key to this is good counsel. You need to be honest and express your pain to the right people. People who will listen and empathize, but in the end will tell you the truth about your own behavior and what God would call you to do in those situations.

Don't just vent and listen to the person sitting closest to you and assume you will be getting sound advice. Choose your people very carefully with forethought. Choose people you look up to that will give you their guidance in a way that is not just agreeing with you or will just regurgitate what they might do. Do choose people who will empathize with you and then help show you what God's word says about your particular situation.

After receiving good counsel there are further steps. No person knows what you should do in a given situation, especially if you don't even know. After getting human counsel, you need to pray about it. You need to take it to a place where you can get all your answers. You need to ask God for His guidance and direction on what you should do in the situation. Journaling can help with getting the situation out and expressing your hurt and pain. It can help get you to the point of being able to hear God on the matter. Then you will truly have His plan, not just a plan of what the world would have you do.

**THIRD** - take action. Do not sit around thinking about your situation. Get out of yourself and your situation by finding a way to be a blessing to someone else. It could be taking a meal to a neighbor, or babysitting for a friend. It can be anything - just spend some time thinking about someone else and helping to meet their need.

This will get you off your own mind for awhile. In the process it will bring perspective. It will give God some time to work on your mind and your situation and give you a chance to bless someone else in their time of need. Both great things.

**FOURTH** - examine your part in the situation. Yes, you may suffer without fault at times in your life, though this is rarely the case. We usually have some part to play in our own troubles. We always have something to learn about ourselves. If we are open to what God is showing us, we can learn something to make our lives better. Even if we don't like to admit it, we usually have played a part in a troubling situation.

We need to be willing to take these situations to God and ask Him how we can better handle things. We need to ask ourselves what our parts in the situation(s) are so we don't have to learn the lesson again. This process of continually looking for our part is very important and will be a key for pulling out of our struggles. As we examine ourselves more and more, we will see that we play a major role in our own struggles. The reasons these situations are struggles is because of the way we look at them. If our thoughts are on the right track, the struggles will be less and less.

This is not meant to be a session of beating yourself up. You may not be primarily responsible for the situation, but if we can find out our part, no matter how little it might be, we will improve our responses in future situations.

**FIFTH** - remember how much God has forgiven us. There are times we suffer without any fault of our own. Those times can be especially difficult. I did everything right. I did everything I was supposed to do but a situation or person still caused deep pain. In these times we need to think back to Jesus. He suffered without ANY fault in ANYTHING.

We may be blameless in any particular situation, but there are plenty of situations where we have not been blameless and have not had to suffer the consequences. Ask God to help you to forgive and let go of the situation. We will talk more on this topic later.

In summary – struggles are really just opportunities that we are presented with. Challenges and struggles seem all consuming and overwhelming in the moment, but they are really just opportunities. We make them negative or positive. Assigning those titles to our struggles comes through our reaction to them. There is a choice in there for us.

One choice is to stay in the bitterness and anger toward the person or situation. This is one way to go with the situation. The other way would be to look for the lessons in the situations for our own growth and offer forgiveness where needed to others.

We need to think about situations and remember the bigger picture. We are only here on Earth for a very short time. All that "matters" or makes a real difference here is what we do for God and others, not ourselves. Don't get stuck in your emotions.

*Here are some examples of how to rethink struggles:*

- They give us opportunities to realize changes that need to be made in us, not judgments to make of others.
- They give us the chance to remember that we do not have all the knowledge needed to judge, but that God will judge and take care of the situations for us.
- They give us opportunities to dig deep in ourselves, see our problems, read God's word, and gain more knowledge of Him in this situation and in our lives overall.
- They give us opportunities to extend grace and remember all the grace that has been extended by other people and most of all by God to us. Remember every person needs that same grace and none of us deserve it.
- There are also great ways to change our thinking to help us overcome struggles but there are other things that keep us stuck. Let's look at a few of those.

## #1 KEY TO GETTING OUT OF OUR STRUGGLES

Want to know the secret for getting out of struggles? Are you ready for this? You may not like it, but the number one key to getting out of struggles is forgiveness.

That's it. Simple, right? Just forgive EVERYONE and you will be free from struggles. Yeah right. A lot easier said than done.

If we don't forgive we are walking on dangerous ground. Matthew 6:9-15 gives us the Lord's Prayer. Jesus is teaching the disciples the best way to pray and there is only one contingency in that prayer. "Father forgive us our sins as I forgive those who sin against me." That means that whatever measuring stick we use against others to judge whether or not they should be forgiven, is the same stick that God will use against us.

What? Say that again. If I don't forgive, I'm not forgiven? This is a powerful statement. How are we living it out in our lives?

Remember, we need to examine our lives. If we fully examine ourselves, we will realize that we need a lot of forgiveness. If you don't think you do, your biggest problem is pride. Pride in that, "I am good and in fact better than most." Pride in that, "I am good all on my own." But if we honestly examine ourselves we know we need liberal forgiveness for things we know we have done wrong and for things we don't even realize we have done wrong. Therefore, we'd better offer that same liberal standard to others, because if we do not, we won't be given those same liberal standards of forgiveness either.

I know, I know, you might say: "But you don't know what they did to me. They are spreading rumors and lies about me. They sexually abused me. They took advantage of me financially and I am ruined. Horrible things have happened to me - I was raped. I was physically abused." The list could go on and on.

I realize and sympathize. It is hard.

I've had to forgive similar things in my life. But, holding onto the hurt, whatever the hurt, is not helping you. Whatever you are stewing about is probably not hurting the person that hurt you much at all. You are the one holding onto the emotional charge of the situation. They are off living life footloose and fancy free. (This is not to say that they will get away with it, it is only to say YOU are not the one who will bring judgment upon them.) And by holding onto the situation, you are the one suffering. By holding onto the situation YOUR life is being compromised, damaged, and this is less than what God would want for you.

So with that as the backdrop, I hope you are willing and can then realize that it doesn't matter what has been done to you. Forgiveness is the only way out of the situation and struggle.

I do not say this as though it is easy to do. I know it's hard and feels unfair. But it is possible and it is the only way to be set free from our struggles.

## A "TO DO" LIST TOWARD FORGIVENESS

There are many ways to find forgiveness. I will share some of the thinking processes and later we will look at some specific activities that have worked for me in this journey. Use this as a starting point, but go where God is taking you. Not everyone will find forgiveness in exactly the same way but we ALL can find forgiveness, no matter the situation.

For me the forgiveness process starts with minute by minute forgiveness. I have to push out the negative, consuming thoughts over and over and over again. And forgiving doesn't mean forgetting. The situation or person will keep coming to mind, but it is our job to remind ourselves that God will take care of it and we want to live a full life for ourselves.

By letting go of the desire to pass judgment, you will be freeing yourself. It will simply lose its control over you. The emotional charge can "slowly-by-slowly" (common Kenyan phrase) be removed from you and be replaced by the wonderful work God wants you to do!

"But they don't deserve forgiveness for what THEY did." That may be true, they might not deserve it. But this is inherent in the definition of forgiveness. If the person being forgiven deserved it, it would not be labeled forgiveness. Forgiveness always goes to those who don't deserve it. Remember, we do not deserve forgiveness, but we receive it.

Therefore, no matter the situation, we need to forgive. This NEED is about us, not about the other person. Forgiving lets us off the hook to personally hold them accountable for their actions. Forgiveness leaves it up to God to punish and handle the situation. That leaves us free for wonderful works and a shiny new life, untainted by the actions or inactions of others.

Some people speak of forgiveness as a get-out-of-jail-free card. That may be true, but not for the person who you think. Forgiveness doesn't let people off the hook who have done wrong. They are still accountable to God, who is the only one who can truly judge them and their actions. They are not getting out of jail free. YOU are. Forgiveness actually lets you off the hook. You are not responsible for watching them, complaining about them, forcing them, or enforcing them. You give that responsibility over to God and it frees YOU. You are the one that gets out of jail. A jail that you have held yourself in by holding onto bitterness, resentment, and revenge.

That freedom of space in your mind, and your time and energy, leaves room in your life for other things; the projects God has for you, the purpose He has for you. While you are stuck enforcing the rules on someone else, you are not available for those things. Forgiveness is a free pass for US to get out of jail free. Will you take it today?

## A STORY OF FORGIVNESS

There is a story in Genesis that talks about great forgiveness for other people. A story about forgiving people who don't deserve forgiveness. It's the story of Joseph. (Genesis, Chapters 37-50). Joseph was one of the youngest sons of Jacob. Jacob gave Joseph special attention and special privileges because he was younger and because of his special love for Joseph's mom, Rachel. Joseph and the Amazing Technicolor Dream Coat is a musical based on a special coat Joseph received from his father. The other brothers were annoyed by this special attention. To add insult to injury, one day Joseph shared with his brothers that he had a dream. Joseph told his brothers that in his dream they were bowing down to him.

This was the last straw. The brothers were angry. They all went for a hike in the wilderness tending to their animals. Joseph stayed back with his father. At some point Jacob sent Joseph out to check on his brothers. When the brothers saw Joseph approaching, their anger was rekindled, so they decided they were going to kill him and throw him into a well. But then they changed the plan and decided to sell him into slavery so they could make a little money on the deal. They went home and told their father, Jacob, that they thought Joseph was killed by an animal and showed his bloody coat as proof.

So the brothers made money selling Joseph into a life of misery as a slave and then lied to their dad about it. Joseph could have thrown in the towel and ranted and raved about the fact that his brothers were horrible people and had no right to do this to him. They should be put in their place.

But instead Joseph kept busy, and worked his way up into a better situation. During his time in slavery, Joseph showed himself to be faithful and earned the right to be the household help for the second highest man in Egypt, Potiphar. Even in undeserved slavery, God was with him. Things were going well for him. He stayed focused on the positives and kept moving forward without looking back with bitterness and anger.

Then Potiphar's wife, who was attracted to Joseph, wanted him to sleep with her. He again and again refused out of respect to his boss and more importantly to God. He refused her advances. Finally, one day the only people in the house were Joseph and Potiphar's wife. She again makes an advance and pulls at his robe. He runs away from her to get out of the situation. In doing that, she pulls his robe off, and then cried out that he tried to rape her. Potiphar removes him from his house, which is bad enough, but also throws him in jail.

So first his brothers sell him into slavery and then Potiphar's wife has him thrown into prison even though he was completely innocent. He was doing the right thing and yet bad things kept happening to him. But Joseph doesn't have a bad attitude. He stays focused on obeying his authorities everyday, and focuses on the positives. He again works his way up within the prison system by continually doing the right thing. He gets to the point that even though he was a prisoner, he was in charge of all the other prisoners. He was that trustworthy and reliable. God was with Joseph and he acted accordingly.

After several years, some of Pharaoh's servants end up in the prison with him – a cupbearer and a baker. One night, both of the servants had a dream. Joseph was able to interpret the dreams correctly and they were both very grateful to him. In the dream one of the men was to be restored to his position with Pharaoh. Joseph begged them, "Don't forget me when you get back to Pharaoh's palace!" Years went by. Joe was long forgotten again.

How many opportunities did Joseph have to throw in the towel? Give up on himself? Give up on God? Yet again and again he kept moving forward in faith, knowing God was with him. He continued to do the right thing. He did not stay stuck in bitterness over the wrongs done to him by his brothers, or the lies by Potiphar's wife, or even being forgotten by those he spent time to help. He kept doing the right thing.

Finally, years later, the Pharaoh had a dream. After Pharaoh exhausted all the normal people he used to interpret dreams there was still no resolution and he was tormented. Finally, the cupbearer remembered Joseph who had interpreted a dream for him all those years ago in prison. He told Pharaoh about Joseph, and Pharaoh demanded Joe's presence. This was not because Pharaoh trusted him, but because he had run out of other options. So Joseph cleaned himself up and was brought before Pharaoh.

To make a long story short, Joseph interpreted the dream, and because he was able to do so, Pharaoh put him as second in command of the entire nation of Egypt. The dream indicated that Egypt and the entire region would have seven years of plenty and then seven years of famine. Based on Pharaoh's dream, Joseph laid out a plan to prepare Egypt for the lean times ahead.

Overnight, Joseph received a wife, sons, servants, chariots and anything else his heart desired. He was in charge of the entire country and savings hundreds of thousands of lives. He quickly went from prison to the palace. How did this happen? Because he kept his focus on always doing the right thing, even when the right thing was not being done to him.

Joseph continued to serve in the palace for many, many years. The years of plenty pass, and the time of famine arrives. One day, as he was doing the right thing in his position of power, minding his business, who should show up to beg for food? None other than Joe's long lost brothers. Remember those guys, the ones who sold him into slavery? What did he do then? Did he sink into bitterness over what they had done and the downward spiral it caused? I'm sure Joe was tempted. I'm sure the memories came flooding back like a flashback scene in a movie. Joseph's reaction toward them showed an internal struggle, but he had forgiveness in his heart.

## PURPOSE IN STRUGGLES

Joseph's family and the entire Jewish community were without food because of the famine. Joseph saved Egyptians, his family, and all the Jewish people from starvation, through HIS struggles. If it was an Egyptian in that position of power, the food would probably have been saved for only the Egyptians, leaving the Jewish community to die.

So even though we are in the middle of struggles and we may not know why -- God always has a reason for things. Had he not been in prison Joseph would not have been in a position to save his family and all his people from starvation. It was only because of what his brothers did, and what Potiphar's wife did, that Joseph was able to be in the position where God needed him, as second in command of Egypt.

If you push through, you will see many of God's reasons for doing things the way that He does them in your own lifetime. For some of them it will take getting to heaven to see why, but either way, we can rest assured our struggles are not without a purpose. The question is, "Are we willing to push through the forgiveness process to find out or will we stay stuck in bitterness and resentment?"

It took a few steps. Those were not easy years for Joseph, and it was not easy to keep bitterness at bay, but he did. Because he did God was able to bless him more than he could ever have imagined. What his brothers meant for evil . . . God used for Joseph's good and the good of all the Jewish people.

Joseph's story shows us how our struggles, especially our struggles to forgive, are not just meant for us, but also to help others around us. If Joseph had fallen into bitterness instead of choosing forgiveness, the entire Nation of Israel could have died out from starvation. Because Joseph did not fall into bitterness, but instead chose forgiveness and Israel was saved.

Our struggles are not only meant for us. They are meant to help other people too. People who see us walk through the struggles, people we share our struggles with. People who see us on the other side. People who read about struggles in our books or articles. We need to share our struggles and let others help us and allow our struggles to help others.

## PERSONAL STORY OF FORGIVENESS

I remember a struggle I once had with a Christian leader and mentor. We had been working on a nonprofit together to get it up off the ground. She was the founder and executive director. I did the legal work to obtain the 501(c)(3) tax status and was asked to be the President of the board. I accepted. I worked my butt off day and night to get the nonprofit to the next level doing whatever activity was asked of me and coming up with other activities as well. At one point, I had to turn all the work over to some-one because I was going to be out of town for 10 days.

When I returned, I was asked to leave the board because "people were complaining about me", and it was not working out. I was hurt. While I was helping and doing most of the work along with the executive director, the rest of the board was doing very little. Even the little work they volunteered to do at meetings somehow never got done.

I felt, "how dare they ask me to leave!" The "removal" process was not handled in a Godly way. There were unfounded accusations and there were very few who were looking at themselves or objectively looking at situations.

I knew God would want me to forgive, but it hurt so bad. I poured myself into this organization and had given my all to it. I was kicked to the curb, left by the side of the road, with false accusations. People did not handle the situation as the Bible would have called them to. Instead they threw me under the bus without any discussions or self-examination. How unfair. How ungodly! How ungrateful!

I remember during those moments right after the event, there was a minute by minute process of forgiveness. It was constantly on my mind and in my heart. The hurt was so deep. This was a Christian leader someone who brought me close with God. How could she do this to me? How could I have invested so much and then be left out? I didn't understand and I felt it was not right or Godly.

One of the things that I vowed was that I was not going to pull this organization or the people involved through the mud with me. As much as I wanted to, and from my perspective they deserved to be, I knew that was not what God wanted. It was so hard not to talk about the situation. It was consuming my mind, but I did not go on about it. I had two close Christian friends that I would vent to, but that was it. I would not talk about it with anyone else.

It was hard, but within a few weeks of my solid commitment it got a lot easier. The thoughts came through my mind a little less often. Maybe once an hour instead of once a minute. As the days and weeks passed, it was just maybe once in the morning and once at night, and then just once in awhile.

By keeping my mouth shut about what they did wrong, God was able to show me what I had done wrong in the situation. Though none of the accusations they were throwing around were true, it was true that I did not pray about taking on the position of President in this organization. God had called me to help them with the legal work of getting started and I just accepted the appointment through excitement, but without prayer.

Also, my work with that organization was distracting me from my Kenya work. In fact, this had happened in March and I was supposed to go to Kenya in May. By early April, I had not even booked a ticket and I was planning on cancelling the trip so I could help this other organization. So by constant effort of keeping the focus on me and my actions, God was able to show me things that I needed to see and learn from. If I was still focusing solely on them and "what they did to me", I would never have seen my part in this and what it was I was sacrificing.

Leaving the story there would be enough of a forgiveness story, but God had another plan. Around July of that same year, God, in a moment while I was vulnerable, moved me to reach out to this person again.

I remember the exact moment it came up. I was on a plane to Kenya in July with Brooklyn and her friend Josie. We were on the airplane and I was having one of those moments of unexplainable crying that I sometimes get (Always love those moments when they are on an airplane!). I felt God say "Reach out to Amy."

I thought He was nuts. It's hard enough to forgive at a distance and God helped me through that. By this time, I was praying for her and the ministry they were continuing and I was pretty proud of myself for that. It wasn't easy. But now I have to reach out to her and possibly be rejected or hurt again?! That's too much.

But I did what God asked. I reached out. We had a few Bible studies together and have encouraged each other for many years since. I was able to be there for her through some major events in her life when she needed someone with my knowledge and skills, and she has been there for me when things seemed to be falling apart.

Forgiveness is hard, but it does work, and it's worth it. It frees us to see what we need to see about ourselves and also to receive our own forgiveness for our miss-steps.

## LETTING GO OF YOUR OWN MISTAKES

The previous stories are all examples of forgiving others, but I find sometimes, especially with addictions, the first person we need to let off the hook is ourselves.

You have screwed up. Maybe it's drugs or alcohol that have affected not only you, but your entire family. Maybe it's a life of crime, an abortion, many sexual partners. Whatever it was, it's over.

The "crime" is over. What are you going to do now? Keep repeating the same mistakes/patterns over and over again? Why? Because that's what you deserve for what you did? This is certainly one choice and one we make quite often. Punishing and shaming ourselves into the same harmful patterns over and over. That is not going to help, but we chose that often.

Thank God we don't have to take what we deserve. We ALL deserve to suffer and die. We are not perfect people. We make mistake after mistake (both known and unknown). We hurt people purposefully and by accident. We fall short of others' expectations and our own. We are not good enough.

This is not news to God. He knows. That's why he sent Jesus for us. Let's rely on Him and use Him to help us through these situations instead of staying stuck in the muck and mire. The way to start the journey is to ask Him into your heart, thank Him for what He has done, and ask Him to lead you in this process.

Take a moment to do that now. Here is something you might say: "Jesus, I ask you to come along side me and guide me through this life. I have made mistakes and I lay those all before you now. You know every one of my mistakes and I thank you for being here with me now and helping me past them to be closer to You. I believe Jesus lived on this earth, He died, and He rose again to help us lead a life through you." There are no magic words, you just pray what is in your heart. God knows. Saying this prayer and meaning it brings the Holy Spirit to help us!

For those of us who have been on this journey for awhile, we need to remember He died for ALL our sins, not just the ones prior to accepting Him. "While we were still sinners, Christ died for us." (Romans 5:8) He died for ALL, before and after inviting Him into our heart. He knew all we would do, for good or for bad, long before we entered this world and came to the point of committing our first sin. He knew this before the world even began.

It's no surprise to Him, so confess your sin and leave it with Jesus. Don't keep carrying it around with you. It is finished. Jesus has taken care of the bill for your sin with what He did for you on the cross. Let's leave it there for Him and move on already. The first steps toward a new life are accepting the forgiveness from God.

## EXAMPLE OF PERSONAL FORGIVENESS

There's a great story in the Bible we can use as an example of this personal forgiveness. The story of David shows a great level of forgiveness. It is located in 2 Samuel chapters 11-12. David had an affair, which resulted in a pregnancy, and then he killed the lady's husband to cover it up. This man David killed was also one of his best friends, and a high ranking officer in his army. Of course, this was only after trying nicer ways of dealing with it, which didn't work out because the man David killed was so honorable. Then David married his best friend's wife and had a baby with her.

It took close to one year for David to even begin to recognize all the madness that had transpired at his hand. Finally, a dear, trusted friend, the prophet Nathan, shared a story with David. Through this story, David was reprimanded for everything that he had done. Stuff he was ignoring and not acknowledging was brought out into the open. David admitted what he had done to Nathan and to God.

Once David acknowledged his sin, he repented to God for everything. He prayed, fasted, and called on God over and over. He chose to no longer stay in the shame and guilt over the events and all he had done. He acknowledged what he did and repented to God, and then he moved on. He left the drama behind and moved forward with his life. He accepted God's forgiveness and trusted in it. He did not continue with the drama, he continued in God's grace and forgiveness for HIM.

One of David's sons with this woman was Solomon. Solomon was the richest and wisest king ever. If the first situation had ended differently, Solomon may never have been born. God can work bad situations together for good if we allow Him the space and time to do it.

Because David was able to let go of his shame and guilt over the previous situations, God was able to bring him another son that did great, great things. If David had stayed buried in the drama of the situation and all that he had done wrong, he would not have been able to see his next steps and lead his son, and many other situations, into greatness after his major life mistakes.

Let's put our major and minor life mistakes behind us. Bring them to God and ask for forgiveness and then leave them there. Stop trying to take them back. Stop trying to make up for them. Stop doing and start believing. Move forward with what God is calling you to do right now. Keep your focus ahead of you, not behind you. Let's commit to forgiveness.

## WHAT IS STANDING IN YOUR WAY?

Lack of forgiveness blocks our way to God. It is always in the way. Even if we don't consciously think about it often, it is there like a pebble or a rock or a boulder blocking the river of God's purposes for you. After a while, with enough boulders and pebbles, the river stops flowing. There is a ton of pressure built up behind the rock, which can lead to anger, self-medicating, physical and emotional illnesses and symptoms, and so many other things.

But the worst part is, you can't be in God's purpose and flow for your life if bitterness, resentment, and lack of forgiveness are blocking the river. We need to let go of the rocks and then the flow of God will return to us. We need to let go of the lack of forgiveness no matter what the situation. Then we can be free to move forward with God.

Are you ready to be in the flow again?

## HOW TO FORGIVE

How do you forgive? Forgiveness means changing our thoughts about a person or a situation. It has very little, if anything, to do with the other person directly.

Here are some things that can help with forgiveness. Again this is not an exhaustive list. This is a starting point.

Look to God through the Bible and spiritual friends for emotional healing.

*Prayer.* Pray about what makes us angry, sad, and hurt. Take all these things to God in prayer and share our feelings with Him.

*Be careful who you share with*. Make sure they're a spiritual friend. Share with a limited number of people. Don't allow yourself to talk about it all the time.

*Look at the person's perspective.* People rarely purposefully hurt us. Try to see the other person's point in the situation even if you don't agree with it. Look to see it. Remember times when we hurt people and were forgiven.

**Look at our part.** Maybe we trusted someone that should not have been trusted. Maybe we were involved in something we should not have been involved with.

**Remember, forgiving does not equal forgetting.** Please do not set yourself up for unreasonable expectations. You do not need to forget the situation ever happened. That will never occur. Forgiveness means you commit to changing your thoughts about the situation. You commit to not letting the situation or person control you anymore. When it comes into your mind, you choose to let it flow right back out of your mind instead of stewing over it.

## FORGIVINESS LETTER EXERCISES

One of the best ways I have found to work through deep-seated pain and come to forgiveness is through this exercise. Write a letter to whomever wronged you.

First, explain everything in the letter. All your hurt and pain. Get all the details out, all the pain and the feelings.

Then in the second half of the letter admit your part in that pain. Express how things might look different from their perspective.

Third, express forgiveness for them. "Because of what Jesus did for me, I let you go from my mind and body. I wish to move forward in my life, free and forgiven for my mistakes. Therefore, I am forgiving you."

After writing these letters I like to burn them, rip them up and throw them in the ocean, or destroy them to represent my letting go of the situation or person and letting God handle it. I cannot go back to it and relive it or read it again and again. This also avoids the letter getting into the wrong hands.

Do not give the letter to the person under any circumstances. First of all, I say this because this letter is about forgiveness for YOU, it is not about them. They don't need to know anything about it.

If you feel you want to share with the person some part of the letter, consult first with a trusted spiritual advisor. It is imperative that we have someone in our lives who we can share things like this with. A spiritual advisor is someone who respects confidentiality, is a straight shooter and totally honest. It could be a Christian friend you have gotten to know over the years and shared your story with, both the good and the bad. Maybe it is your pastor or their spouse. It could be anyone that shares your same spiritual beliefs.

This person needs to be a spiritual advisor, not just anyone. Rework the letter a few times with a person whom you trust and respect. Maybe just a talk with a trusted advisor will help you feel complete.

## FEAR IS AN OBSTACLE TO FORGIVENESS & LIFE

Probably the biggest obstacle to forgiveness and true life is fear. Fear of failure, fear of following wrong direction, fear of the future, fear of the past, fear of disapproval or disappointment, fear of letting people off too easy, etc.

Our society fills us with fear about everything. The news media makes their money selling ads and by selling fear. "Don't let your child be poisoned to death in your house. Watch the 6 o'clock news for details." That is what we are overwhelmed with constantly. It's hard to watch every day and not be pulled in by thoughts filled with fear.

But we do have One that has overcome that fear for us – Jesus. He died on the cross so we could have the power in us to overcome. He wants to walk with us in our fear so we don't have to be afraid, but first we have to let Him in. We have to offer our heart to Him, trust Him, and rely on Him.

We have to put more importance on Him and what He HAS done and less on us and what we are about to do. Remember what He has done calms our fear and helps us to move forward. The Bible says over 365 times (one for every day of the year) "do not be afraid, fear not. Fear not because He is with us." He has the game book. He knows what to do and when to do it. Make your relationship with Him the number one thing in your life and let go of your own thoughts and fears. Replace those thoughts with what God says in His word.

*For example*, at times, that voice in my head tells me how dumb I am and sometimes how dumb other people think I am. "See Carrie you made a mistake again. That person must think you are really stupid." When those thoughts slither into my head, my job is to:

**1.** Be aware of them and how much power I am giving those thoughts in my life, AND

**2.** Replace them with what God says in His word about me. God says I have the mind of Christ. Repeat that over and over.

Sometimes it is hard to find the verses at first, but by heading over to Biblegateway.com and typing in a search word, you can find a verse to replace your own thoughts. After you do this again and again it will become second nature and the thoughts won't be able to slither in as much. Write out verses on index cards or Post-It notes and place them all over your house, office, and car to help you keep your focus on the Word, and not on the fear.

### STORY OF OVERCOMING FEAR

This reminds me of a person in the Old Testament, and I absolutely love her story. Esther is her name. Esther was an orphan. She was taken in by her uncle Mordecai. He raised her. A modern-day beauty contest was to be held because the king was looking for a new wife. Esther was gorgeous and was chosen from her small village to be one of the final contestants in this beauty parade. Read the book of Esther in the Bible for the full story which is a really fun, short read. Spoiler alert! Read the story now and enjoy the suspense before I ruin it for you.

Esther was chosen as the king's favorite in the contest. As time progressed, she was living with the king and doing her queenly duties and enjoying her new good fortune and comfort. It was probably well deserved after what was a tough life as an orphan.

One of the king's head advisors, Haman, was disgruntled with Esther's uncle Mordecai. Haman was a power hungry, prideful jerk, to put it nicely. One of the rules that the king and his court had decreed was that all people must bow-down to the king and his court. Mordecai was a Jew and could not or would not bow-down to Haman or anyone else because of his religion. Haman did not like that. It disrespected his power and he was looking for a way to get back at Mordecai because of his failure to bow down to him.

Haman came to the king with a great idea. "King, they are disrespecting us so let's set a date when anyone who wishes to can legally kill any Jewish person they want without fear of penalty. Thereby, we will get rid of all the disobedient people." And Haman adds for good measure, "King, I will donate lots of silver into your treasury if we can do this." Without much thought to it, the king allowed the decree to be issued.

The king was unaware that his queen, Esther, was Jewish. Mordecai and all the Jewish people got word of the decree and they were all very frightened and scared. They wore mourning clothes, they fasted, and they prayed. They did everything they could think of for God to rescue them from the death threat hanging over their heads.

Esther was blissfully unaware of anything that was going on, enjoying her comfortable life in the palace. Uncle Mordecai reached out to her through her servants. Her servants gave her a copy of the decree so she knew exactly what was going on, including the amount of the bribe offered and a message from Mordecai asking that she go to the king and plead with him for her people.

She was scared. She knew she could not go before the king without him asking for her. If she went before the king without permission, the penalty for her was death. She sent back the information to Mordecai saying there was nothing she could do because she would not be called before the king for the next 30 days.

Mordecai responded back stronger. He told Esther, don't think you will escape from this decree. This will come and bite you also. He told her, if you remain silent at this time, you and all the Jews will perish. You need to speak up. His famous closing line is, "Who knows whether you have not attained royalty for such a time as this?" Meaning the whole reason God brought you to the palace was for this purpose - to save the Jews in their time of desperation.

This struck her to the core. Fear paralyzed her. She would be killed if she went before the king without him asking for her. What was she to do? She sent a message back to Mordecai saying assemble the Jews and fast. Do not eat or drink for three days and nights. She and her servants would fast at the same time. "Then I will go before the king, and if I perish, I perish." Bravery.

She took steps even though she was afraid. I won't give away the ending of the story. You will have to go and read the book for that. It is well worth the read.

Bravery, but not because of lack of fear. Inherent in the definition, bravery means there is fear. If there was no fear, one would not need to be brave.

But she did it while she was afraid. That's what we need to do as well. It is ok to be afraid. There is no shame in that. Fear can serve as a warning in some situations, but we cannot let that stop us from what God is calling us to do. If God has called us to do something, we cannot just walk away because the going gets tough or we think the problem won't affect us so we ignore it. We need to stand up and fight for what God has called us to fight for. We cannot let our fear run us out of the ring. We need some strategies to use to walk through fear.

## STRATEGIES FOR WALKING THROUGH FEAR

Here are a few strategies that have worked really well for me during periods of fear:

### READ THE BIBLE.

God's word is powerful. It is the sword of the Holy Spirit *(Ephesians 6:17)*. It is the only offensive weapon we have to bring light to the darkness of this world. We need to know how to use it and we need to use it well. This is the only place where we can find real peace.

The Bible is God's written word to us. It is the place to go to find answers to the questions of life. Commit to reading The Word often. Read at least five days a week for a few minutes each day. Take a few notes as you read. Maybe at first they will be mostly questions, but as you continue, you will begin to find the answers. Using a good study Bible that contains notes will help you answer your questions too.

If you have a specific problem, look up verses with those words in them. For example, if you are fearful, find verses on fear, afraid, etc. Study those verses, read them over and over. Post them in your car, bathroom mirror etc. so you can remember to read them over and over. If you don't know what you need and you feel overwhelmed and don't know where to start, look up the word LOVE. Find all the verses you can on love and write your favorite ones out on an index card and keep them with you and post them around you. A good study Bible will have a concordance and an index to subjects that you can use.

REMEMBER - F.E.A.R = False Evidence Appearing Real

If I don't remember this by heart and catch it early, the fear will run through my mind and take me places I don't want to be. The F.E.A.R acronym is easy to remember, and I have found it very helpful.

The devil uses fear to keep us from reaching our full potential in this world. We are stopped by fear which is exactly what he wants. If we keep in front of us this definition of what FEAR actually is, we are more likely to keep moving forward, in spite of the fear and even at some points, because of it. FEAR is simply - False Evidence Appearing Real. Remember this and it can bring comfort to the next steps.

## DO IT AFRAID.

Another piece of advice I have received through the years is that it is okay to be afraid. You can be afraid. We are all afraid of different things and at various times. There is nothing wrong with this. The problem comes if we feel the fear and run the other way or assume we are on the wrong path. That is a problem. We need to:

## "DO IT AFRAID!"

We need to feel the fear and move forward anyway. After prayer, of course, but we need to still keep moving. Have courage!

Have courage just as Esther did. Don't you think the president of the United States is afraid when he sends our young men and women into war? Does he think, no matter what, this will come out perfect and I have no doubt about that? I know this is the perfect thing to do. No – he is scared out of his mind that this could end up in disaster. Thousands of people could die because of his decision and we could leave the situation defeated like we did in Vietnam and other conflicts along the way. But does that stop him from acting at all? No, he "does it afraid" to protect a higher societal good.

Do you think the mom is afraid to send her little baby to kindergarten at such a big school? Yes, but she does it anyway because she knows in the end it will be a better life for that little one with social interaction and teachers to lead and guide her child. We "do it afraid".

Making decisions to go to Kenya these days is a fearful proposition. Between health threats and security threats, there is fear in lots of ways. But I need to pray He will help me to watch for His signs and guidance before making decisions, and even after decisions have been made.

We have to take action afraid. That is where we will see God do his mightiest works. When we are consumed by fear and surrender control, God can take over and show us amazing things!

Let's do it today! Let's do it afraid and see how God will bless us!

(Read John Ortberg's book *If You Want to Walk on Water, You Have to Get Out Of the Boat*. It talks a lot about fear and other things that keep us stuck. It is a great read and will help you pull through in many areas.)

## WARNING

I hope this book has been a source of encouragement for you on your own journey with God wherever He is taking you. I hope you have learned strategies in dealing with depression, sadness, overwhelming struggles, and so much more. That being said, not all depression and overwhelming struggles can be overcome through thought changes alone.

Though most can be helped through recognizing our own thoughts, some struggles are chemical within our body. Those chemical issues need to be addressed and overcome with the help of a doctor. That is not a reflection of a person's strength or personality. It is simply a reality of our body chemical make-up. Please seek professional help if you think you need it.

## CONCLUSION

In conclusion, I have recently lived through some major life-changing struggles that you will learn more about in my next book. But for now, I can share with you from the bottom of my heart, a heart just brought through the absolute pit of despair, a pit that I didn't know if I would ever come out of again. This stuff works! The answers are in God's Word. The Overcomer has overcome for us. We just need to push on and let Him guide us. Hope has come and is with us – let's rest in that. He is our only hope and He is with us. Rest in Him.

I hope you will continue on this journey with me. There is quite a roller coaster ahead. Let's look forward to see where God leads us. I would also love to hear your story or even share it with you in person through an event with your group. Please be in touch. Let's keep each other encouraged as we live this thing, that is sometimes filled with struggles, called life.

*With love,*
*Carrie 12/2014*

# About Carrie Reichartz, Author

Carrie Reichartz is a lawyer and small business owner in New Berlin, Wisconsin USA, where she was born and raised. She is wife to Chris, mom to Colton and Brooklyn, and step-mom to Lexie and Zach. She graduated from UW-Whitewater with a BS in psychology/criminal justice, and received her law degree from Marquette University Law School in Milwaukee, Wisconsin.

Carrie has always had a passion for working with and for children. She has worked as a guardian ad litem representing children's rights in court as a practicing lawyer for seven years. She has written for several legal publications and, shortly after being voted by her peers as a Rising Stars lawyer, she went to Kenya for the first time on a mission trip with Fox River Christian Church in 2008.

After her return Carrie closed her law office to open a home day care so she could be closer to her children and have more time to work on international issues. Currently she travels to Kenya two to three times per year and is developing a much needed Pregnancy Crisis Center near Mombasa. The first of it's kind. Right now most girls are kicked out of their homes and schools when it is found that they are pregnant. They are left to the streets and prostitution or sex trafficking to feed themselves.

While in Kenya Carrie spends time in orphanages, rescue centers, boys' homes, schools, and more. Interacting with the kids and with the staff, bringing projects to do together and sharing in their talents of music and more. She takes people with her on trips to Kenya as well. (Check out InfinitelyMoreWi.org for more details.)

After the Ebola scare in the media in 2014, Carrie closed her home day care business so she could raise awareness and funds fulltime for the people of Kenya.

She speaks in public and private schools, home school groups, Women's events, civic organizations, libraries, and more. Topics include: "Poverty Around the World", "A Day in the Life of a Woman in Kenya", "How Flip Flops are Bringing People to Christ in Kenya", overcoming trauma and also builds topics around event themes.

# Let's stay connected!

*Thank you for taking your time to experience Kenya with me.
I hope you will continue this journey with God in Kenya.*

Carrie Reichartz – personal page
InfinitleyMoreWi

Carrie Reichartz - author page

Infinitely More Wi

Contact Carrie at <u>KenyaGiveHope@yahoo.com</u>
Subject: READ YOUR BOOK

*2013 Community Day. This is my mom Connie Randlett (left) and myself (right) with a group of children from the community, walking hand in hand. They just want to be near you!*

# Want to make a difference?

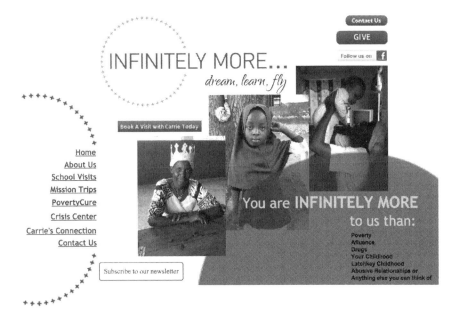

- *Donate today at:* **InfinitelyMoreWI.org**
- Host a fund raising event - Carrie can help you with that!
- Contact Carrie above for volunteer projects available.
- Come with Carrie on a trip – see more details at InfinitelyMoreWI.org

*Speaking for preschool
through adults*

# Carrie is available to speak to you and your group or school

Topics vary "Poverty Around the World", "A Day in the Life of a Woman in Kenya", "How Flip Flops are Bringing People to Christ in Kenya". Carrie can build a topic around your theme.

School presentations include "A Day in the Life of Edgar a Kenyan Child" from shopping to shoes, school, to shelter. We will talk about our lives and what life is like for a child in Kenya and how to make a difference!

Go to InfinitelyMoreWi.org to book your event today!

..................................................................................................

# Where the journey began Book 1

Available at Amazon in paperback or at OperationGiveHope.Etsy.com

*Audio version of the book is available as well*

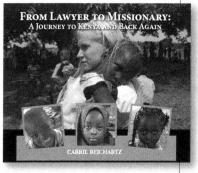

*Coming soon...*

Children's book: *Do the Leaves Change Color in Kenya Too?*
...teaching Kenyan culture, Swahili colors and more!

# Help us support local Kenyan women selling their "curios".

## Visit OperationGiveHope.Etsy.com

Purchase some of their items – paper beaded necklaces,
other jewelry, prints made out of pieces of banana trees, bags and purses,
nativity sets hand-carved, and so much more. Items change constantly!

### *Unique, one-of-a-kind gifts that save lives of women and their families!*

*All proceeds from these sales go back to Kenya to save the lives of pregnant girls and their babies!*

Made in the USA
Columbia, SC
13 May 2020